Hamilton Carhartt

in Rock Hill, South Carolina
"Where the sweet Catawba flows and where the staple cotton grows."

Founder of Carhartt Clothing
Creator of Bib Overalls

Researched and Written by Pat Grant

Hamilton Carhartt

in Rock Hill, South Carolina
"Where the sweet Catawba flows and where the staple cotton grows."

Founder of Carhartt Clothing
Creator of Bib Overalls

Researched and Written by Pat Grant

Hamilton Carhartt in Rock Hill, South Carolina

Founder of Carhartt Clothing
Creator of Bib Overalls

His Mills, Plantation, and English Village
in Rock Hill, South Carolina

Researched and Written
by

Pat Hollis Grant
963 Normandy Way
Rock Hill, South Carolina 29732
803-372-1315
pathollisgrant@cs.com

For my Family
Connie, Lori
Caroline, Jess, Anderson
Sarah McCain, Jonathen, Elena, Aria, Preston
Jeb, Jubal, Scarlett, Lila
in Memory of Phillip

Preston Hollis Sanders

My Great-Grandchildren:
Anderson Grant
Preston, Elena, and Aria Sanders

Anderson Helms Grant

Hamilton and Annette Carhartt
Photo Courtesy of Gary Williams

"Hamilton Carhartt is a man of charming personality, with the most beautiful
manners, clearly marking him as a cultured man of the world.
He is a prince in every sense of the word, full of the Chivalry of the South
and the Ginger of the North."
Detroit Banker, 1907

CONTENTS

FOREWARD   xi

PREFACE   xiii

ACKNOWLEDGMENTS   xv

INTRODUCTION   1

CARHARTT BRAND   5

CARHARTT COMPANY STANDARDS   11

HAMILTON CARHARTT COTTON MILLS IN ROCK HILL
    Hamilton Carhartt Mills No. 1   25
    Hamilton Carhartt Mills No. 2   43

CARHARTT PLANTATION   53
    Mansion   56
    Farm   65
    Arabian Stallion Breeding Program   69
    Jones Grist Mill, Carhartt Electrical/Grist Mill   73
    The 1916 Great Flood   81

CARHARTT'S ENGLISH VILLAGE   93
    Lynderboro Street   98

LAND TRANSACTIONS   99

CARHARTT AFTER ROCK HILL   107

WORKS CITED   109

APPENDIX
    The Hamilton Carhartt Family   111
    Newspaper Articles Relating to Hamilton Carhartt   127

ABOUT THE AUTHOR   167

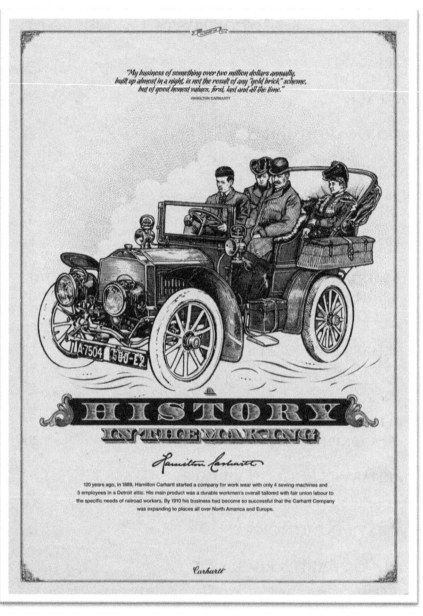

Hamilton and Annette Carhartt on passenger side.
(Driver on right side.)

FOREWORD

HISTORIC
ROCK HILL

I grew up on the north side of Rock Hill in the 1960's and 70's - not far from Red River Road. There was a small "mill village" that backed up to the massive modern Celanese Plant. Across the road was a small factory built by the American Icon; Hamilton Carhartt. The small factory was then called Randolph Yarns. It never dawned on me that this was one of "THE" Hamilton Carhartt's handful of factories he had across the US in the early 20th century. Also, lost behind the massive chain linked fence that encircled the Celanese property, laid the ruins of a luxurious mansion that Hamilton Carhartt built overlooking a bend in the Catawba River.

During my youth, the City of Rock Hill was going through its now detested 1970's version of "Urban Renewal." We saw new buildings replacing old ones, modern four lane roads replacing whole business districts, and a roof was being considered to put over Main Street. However, Red River Road was not included. It had become a neglected and forgotten part of our community.

On Friday nights in the 1980's, we high schoolers would gather at the Putt Putt Course on Celanese Road owned by Gary Williams. Our routine was to load up and ride the short distance to see if we could see the supposed "ghosts" that lived on Lynderboro Street off Red River Road. The road was spooky! It was a dark dirt road with trash all over the place. We slowed down with flashlights and shined them on these strange houses with round porches and "eerie" symbols etched on the sides. Each house looked about the same. Some were occupied and some abandoned. But they were all run down and neglected. Looking for a cheap and spooky thrill, we had no clue that we were at one of the most historic areas in all of York County.

Since then, both Celanese and Randolph Yarns have gone away and have been replaced with today's version of urban renewal - warehouse and residential development. The area is totally unrecognizable today from what I remember growing up. However, in 2005 when the Celanese "chain link fence" came down, the area opened up. Pat Grant was able to expand her extensive research. She turned "folklore" into facts. Thanks to her, I have come to better realize the significance of those strange houses along that dark and spooky road and the significance of those ruins of a mansion that towered over the banks of the Catawba River. I have also come to realize the historical importance of this entire area. Her work culminates with this book. I hope you enjoy it as much as I have.

I also want to thank Jennifer Sandler, Historic Rock Hill's Executive Director. She and her husband Bryan Ghent took Pat's work and turned it into this accessible publication. Historic Rock Hill seeks to preserve and promote the collective history of Rock Hill, so this book perfectly fits our mission and vision. Historic Rock Hill is proud to help Pat get this book in your hands.

Chip Hutchison
Historic Rock Hill
Board Chair

PREFACE

My passion is history. I speak on York County history in classrooms, clubs, and churches; lead walks to historic sites; and film TV programs on history for Betty Jo Rhea's <u>City Minute</u> on CN3 in Rock Hill. Years ago, someone asked me about an English Village that was once in Rock Hill. I started digging into old newspapers, deeds, plats, maps, and everything else that I could find. I found Hamilton Carhartt on paper but no physical evidence of Hamilton Carhartt. My life took a new direction.

How could a man who was such a force for good in Rock Hill not be common knowledge among the citizens? I became determined to make his life well-known in Rock Hill and to ensure his legacy. As I started classes on his contributions to Rock Hill and leading walks to the foundational remains of his plantation and the one remaining English Cottage, I learned that others did not know that Hamilton Carhartt, the founder of Carhartt Clothing and creator of bib overalls, had a life in Rock Hill for nearly two decades. He put Rock Hill on the world map by advertising his denim overalls as Made in Rock Hill, South Carolina. He bred Arabian horses and listed Rock Hill, South Carolina, on records in the <u>Arabian Stud Book</u>.

I believe that Hamilton Carhartt was building a second home for himself and family on the bank of the Catawba River. Why else would you build concrete posts for farm pasture? The expectation in York County was that the area known as Carhartt Station and Carhartt, South Carolina, would grow into a town. The first written and verbal history of the area states that the area was a trading crossroads. According to an article in <u>The Evening Herald</u> on 7 February 1920, Mr. Carhartt was addressing the need to have a modern railroad station with telegraphic services for visitors who were beginning to come. Carhartt Station was described as a simple shed to protect one from the rain. Louise Pettus stated in an article in the <u>York Enquirer</u> on 23 March 2003, that by 1920 Hamilton Carhartt was spending most of his time on his model plantation on the Catawba River. The story goes that as long as Mr. Carhartt lived, he thought of his plantation along the Catawba River as the most restful place he had ever seen, a place of peace.

Rock Hill, <u>The Evening Herald</u>, February 7, 1920

Mrs. Fred W. Brooks Jr. of Detroit, Michigan, daughter of Senator Truman H. Newberry, is a guest of Mrs. Wylie W. Carhartt at the Carhartt Bungalow.

The sharp decline in manufactured goods during the 1920-1921 Global Recession forced many manufacturers in America and Europe to close. Carhartt had to close his two mills in Rock Hill but held on to mills in Atlanta, Detroit, and Dallas. He and his family survived the Global Recession and the Great Depression to continue producing work clothing, street clothing, and iconic wear. Additional information on the Global Recession is included in the chapter on Carhartt Mills.

This book will give you a mind's-eye view of the layout of his plantation, the beauty of the mansion and houses, and the unique design of the English Village and cottages. He first had to build the infrastructure then his plantation and village. This was 1907 through 1921, a time without roads, available water, or electricity. He generated the electricity for his plantation for a number of years. The working- and home-living benefits that Carhartt provided for his employees were mostly dreams for other mill workers in York County.

The research road has been both rewarding and frustrating. Rewarding in July 2010 when tromping through the woods with a friend, we found the foundational remains of the mansion. Frustrating in that I have searched for years for simple facts only to learn that the information was not in the places that I searched. Locating pictures has been the most difficult. Historic Rock Hill has the only picture of the mansion that I could find. This picture has barbed wire strung across the front blocking access to the mansion, and the property was overgrown with weeds indicating the picture was made after the mansion was sold. I chose not to use that unclear picture as it did not represent the mansion and grounds as described in all other sources. I searched records at the county level and all other places that pictures might exist. Luckily, those people who had pictures relating to Carhartt's time in Rock Hill were willing to share them for this book. Now they will be preserved for everyone to see.

Through this research, I found several misstatements that have been carried down through the decades in articles in York County newspapers and other publications. Further research provided more facts than were known 100 years ago; statements have been corrected. I have researched all available sources known to me to provide an accurate account of Carhartt's contributions to our town and to create an awareness of his character, values, and company standards.

Except for the foundational ruins of some of the buildings at the plantation site, there is no evidence and little knowledge of Hamilton Carhartt's years in Rock Hill. The next effort is working with Zach Lemhouse of the Historical Center of York County and Chip Hutchison of Historic Rock Hill to erect a Historical Marker recognizing Hamilton Carhartt's years in Rock Hill. Though Carhartt's architectural contributions have not been preserved, I have attempted to capture and preserve his input into the betterment of Rock Hill and Rock Hill's people.

Never have I read of a man who cared to such an extent about the quality of the goods manufactured at his mills and who gave his employees benefits beyond their expectations. A role model in all ways.

**To know the character of Hamilton Carhartt
is to lift your viewpoint of humanity.**

ACKNOWLEDGMENTS

Historic Rock Hill added the finishing touches to this book to bring the facts and stories of Hamilton Carhartt's years in Rock Hill to the community. Deep thanks to Jennifer Sandler, Executive Director of Historic Rock Hill, Bryan Ghent, and Martha Ghent for proofing this book and making suggestions to make the book more readable. They gave their time and shared their expertise in bringing this book to print.

Paul Gettys has dedicated decades to historic research and preservation. He freely shares his deep-dug facts plus subject-related bits and pieces to enhance an article or book. The history of York County would be thin if it were not for Paul Gettys and the late fellow historian Louise Pettus. Thank you.

Betty Hill Rankin, on a walk along the Riverwalk Trail, gave me printed information on the Arabian horses that Carhartt bred on his farm including a picture of Carhartt's internationally known foundation Arabian horse, Houran. Betty has enriched this book with her knowledge of Arabian horses. She was gracious and generous with her time to research and add facts to the section on Arabian horses and to proof my retype. She located non-local newspaper articles that are now included in this book.

Chip Hutchison, in a last-minute effort to save the remaining cottage of the English Village, rang the final bell to all who might come forth to save and preserve. The remaining cottage was razed in April 2021. I regularly checked the status of the cottage and learned that it was two to three weeks away from destruction. Chip immediately became involved with Luxpoint, a company that offers 3D Laser Scanning, to measure both inside and outside of the cottage. He is working with Winthrop University's History Department to produce a small-scale version of the cottage and we hold a dream of recreating a full-sized replica with a utilitarian purpose for the public.

Gary Williams for his input and suggestions with the Carhartt Mill chapter and providing great pictures for this book. Mostly, for his support in this effort to preserve Rock Hill's history.

Mary Mallaney shared the most unexpected pictures of the Carhartt Plantation during the 1916 Great Flood. An unbelievable addition to this book. Mary researched and helped me to understand (somewhat) the legal use of trademarks, copyrights, and the public domain.

Caroline Grant, my granddaughter, for giving her time, talent, skill, and patience to turn dark "No-See-Ums" pictures into lighter-brighter photos of interest and beauty. Life is easier when you have smart grandchildren.

Zach Lemhouse, Historian, Culture and Heritage Museums of York County and Director of Southern Revolutionary War Institute, for his future guidance and direction in the process to obtain a Historical Marker for the Carhartt Plantation area.

Rylee Aquilant, Leigh Van Blarcom, and Zach Lemhouse for their help in research at the McCelvey Center and for answering my many questions.

Totty Wilkerson is the head cheerleader in the effort to preserve the legacy of Hamilton Carhartt. She spreads the word as she goes through her daily life. She reached out to avenues of possibilities to locate pictures and printed information from the decades of Carhartt's residence in Rock Hill. She is an inspiration in history preservation.

John Skardon, Reference/Genealogy, York County Main Library, not only helps in locating related materials for your research but also independently searches for information. He patiently answers questions and provides direction to all who ask. When traveling the road marked "research," John Skardon is the person who can guide you around potholes and keep you safely between the ditches. He has turned the Research Center at the York County Main Library into a showplace. We are fortunate to have him. Thank you.

Rinne Rogers, Register of Deeds, for guiding me through the trove of deeds and plats at the York County Government Center. Her patience with my lack of knowledge is appreciated.

Betty Jo Rhea, through her CN3 City Minute television programs on area history which I was honored to present, has helped to create an awareness among area viewers that once Rock Hill was honored by Hamilton Carhartt's presence. He left beautiful architecture and better living conditions for workers in his two cotton mills.

Jim Keistler of Keistler Engineering Company Inc. brought survey plats of the Celanese property, formerly the Carhartt Plantation, to my house for use in spreading the history of Hamilton Carhartt's presence in Rock Hill.

Ronnie Parrish formerly worked for Matthews and Benfield Excavation Company during some years of the dismantling and burying of the buildings on the Celanese property, formerly Carhartt Plantation. He shared first-hand experiences of that work. He humorously remembered that during the dismantling, many people came to the work site looking for souvenirs from the mansion, houses, or other buildings.

To everyone who shared information while on a walk to the former Carhartt properties or while in a history class about Hamilton Carhartt, I thank you. Thank you to Janice Chism, Bill Rogers, Jan McCoy, David Cash, and Bruce Worchester for helping to identify parts of the mansion. Too many to name have made contributing comments; I deeply thank all.

**Sharing their areas of expertise
greatly enriched this book.**

_____

History in the Making. Hamilton Carhartt
(From Hamilton Carhartt Cotton Mills Advertisement)

One-hundred and twenty years ago, Hamilton Carhartt started a company for work wear with only four sewing machines and five employees in a Detroit attic. His main product was a durable workman's overall, tailored with fair union labor to the specific needs of railroad workers. By 1910, his business had become so successful that the Carhartt Company was expanding to places all over North America and Europe.

Hamilton Carhartt Cotton Mill, Rock Hill, SC
Courtesy of I'm So Rock Hill, Posted by Frankie Green

Hamilton Carhartt Cotton Mill No. 2
Red River/Celriver Road, Rock Hill

INTRODUCTION
Cotton Mills Where Cotton Grows

The Carolinas had a long and arduous process of division from 1729 when the Carolinas were divided into two colonies until the state line survey in 1772, which divided the Carolinas into two states. Present-day York County had previously been a geographical part of four different counties in North Carolina: Bladen, Anson, Mecklenburg, and Tryon.

The 1763 Treaty of Augusta between representatives of the British Crown, King George III of England, and John Stuart, Superintendent of Indian Affairs, and representatives of the Catawba Indians agreed to a grant to the Catawba Indians of a fifteen-mile-square area of land (144,000 acres) along the Catawba River in the South Colony. The great Catawba Indian Chief, King Hagler, had worked with colonial government officials toward a grant of land away from the inroads of the whites. King Hagler was killed and scalped by Shawnees on 5 August 1763, a little over two months before the 1763 Treaty was signed. Douglas Summers Brown states in The Catawba Indians, The People of the River, that although King Hagler was dead, his name was added to the survey map of the Catawba Territory as his life's work was to gain land for the Catawbas. The 1772 state line had to be surveyed around the Catawba Territory putting the then-Tryon, North Carolina, area (present-day York County) into South Carolina. The area was named New Acquisition County, South Carolina. In 1785, the name York County was given to the area. Early settlement of York County was in the center and western areas of the county.

The tri-counties of York, Chester, and Lancaster in South Carolina take their names from the English counties of York, Chester, and Lancaster. When the early settlers came into Philadelphia, they named the tri-county areas in Pennsylvania: York, Chester, and Lancaster. When the settlers came south on the Great Wagon Road, they brought the tri-county names to the Carolinas. The names originated with the War of Roses (1455-1487). The cousins in the Plantagenet Family fought for the rule of England. The symbol of the House of York was a white rose, and the symbol of the House of Lancaster was a red rose. The rose emblems were on their Battle Flags that led them into battles. York, South Carolina, is known as the White Rose City and Lancaster, South Carolina, is known as the Red Rose City.

Rock Hill was developed one-hundred years later than surrounding towns as the now-Rock Hill area was Catawba Indian Territory. The 1763 Treaty prohibited settlers from claiming the land within the Catawba Indian Territory. The Catawba Indians ceded their interest in the 144,000 acres of land by signing the Nation Ford Treaty of 1840. The 1840 Treaty allowed the settlers who had leased land from the Catawba Indians to have their leased land surveyed for state grants in their names. The state of South Carolina neglected to send the 1840 Treaty to the U.S. Congress for ratification as required by law. This failure, among others, led to the Catawba Indian Land Claim that was not settled until 1993.

Catawba Indian Chief Gilbert Blue led the Catawba Indians from poverty to federal recognition during his years as chief from 1973-2007. The Catawba Indians filed a land claim against the federal government for land losses due to the illegal treaty made by South Carolina in 1840 and the failure of the federal government to protect their interest. The federal government settled the land claim in 1993 with cash, federal recognition for the tribe, and other concessions.

The 110-mile Charlotte to South Carolina Railroad came through the area in 1852 and Rock Hill was born. The White Family and the Springs Family were motivational in having the railroad come through this area as they needed a better way to move the area's commerce. The railroad and cotton industry made Rock Hill.

Rock Hill is named for the rocky knoll that was used as a landmark for Indians and early settlers as they traveled. Ebenezer was on the path of the planned Charlotte to South Carolina railroad; however, Ebenezer did not favor a railroad line in their fair land. The engineers moved the rail line two miles east and identified the new spot for the railroad station on the map by writing "rock hill" near the well-known rocky knoll. The Railroad Depot was built there with the first train arriving in 1852. The town grew around the railroad station and became known as Rock Hill, not Ebenezer as first written on the map. The rock hill was leveled.

York County was mostly agricultural in the early days. The soil in the area was excellent to grow cotton. As late as 1820 South Carolina produced more than one-half the nation's cotton and it was the major crop in nearly every county in the state. The railroad station in Rock Hill became a shipping hub for cotton from the surrounding area. Plantations and farms grew cotton and shipped it to the industrial North for processing in their cotton mills.

After the Civil War in 1865, shipping cotton was impossible because bridges and railroad trestles had been destroyed by the Stoneman Raid Campaign as his troops came through the Carolinas. The relationship between North and South was toxic after the Civil War. Southern mill owners decided to build mills where the cotton grew. Northern mill owners began moving to where the cotton grew because of high taxes in the North.

Hamilton Carhartt came to Rock Hill in 1907 looking for a mill to make denim for his bib overalls. He found what he needed in the Rock Hill Cotton Factory. The mill was built in 1880 as Rock Hill's first mill but was in bankruptcy in 1907.

Carhartt began acquiring land in parcels and eventually owned three miles of land on the west side of the Catawba River from the present-day Highway 21 bridge to beyond the present-day Norfolk Southern Railroad trestle. Articles state that he owned about 2,000 acres on-and-off of Red River Road plus the acreage in the Carhartt Mill Village No. 1. He also owned land on the Fort Mill side (east side) of the Catawba River.

2

Carhartt operated two cotton mills in Rock Hill providing work with a pay scale greater than other area mills and with better working and home-living conditions. He elevated mill houses from bare basics to beauty. He contributed unique architecture with his plantation, mansion, and English Village, a rarity in a small southern county of 50,000 people in 1920. The standard of living for mill employees in Rock Hill was improved through night schools, special education classes, opportunities to develop musical talents, wellness care for employees and their children, playgrounds for children, social gatherings, reduced cost of living by selling items at cost in the company store, and by making employees stockholders in the company. It created an environment of working with Carhartt and not for Carhartt. He wrote regular company newsletters praising individuals for their efforts and accomplishments. Carhartt's employees were individual friends to him. They produced the best denim and overalls because they were the most appreciated as well as the best workers.

Carhartt identified his manufactured goods as Made in Rock Hill, South Carolina, giving Rock Hill name recognition in the countries of Carhartt sales: America, Canada, and Europe. He created the world's most durable work clothing in Rock Hill and became a "role model" mill owner by extending boundaries of employee benefits beyond reach for most other mill owners.

**Hamilton Carhartt's presence
was an honor to Rock Hill, South Carolina.**

3

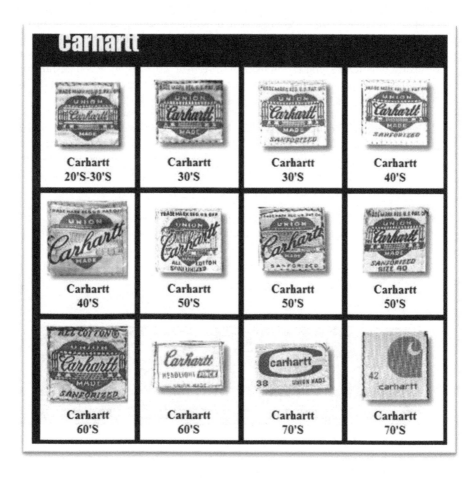

CARHARTT BRAND

"If I can have but one thing, the respect of my customers or
their business, I prefer the former, though I desire both,
and trust I merit them."
Hamilton Carhartt

Hamilton Carhartt founded Carhartt Clothing in 1889 in Detroit, Michigan. He realized a need for ultra-durable clothing for tough working conditions. He worked closely with railroad workers to create a garment that would meet their needs. The bib overall was the completed project. The overalls had a pocket for every tool the railroad workers needed on their jobs. Bib overalls became the ideal work garment not only for railroad workers but also for ranchers, farmers, construction workers, and other tradesmen. Carhartt believed the railroad workers helped him to build his business and he showed his appreciation with contributions throughout his life. He was a supporter of the Home for the Aged and Disabled Railroad Employees of America. His company standards and values created friendship, trust, and respect, which spread from the railroad workers to all who continue to wear the Carhartt Brand. Carhartt set the bar high with his overalls as standard work wear.

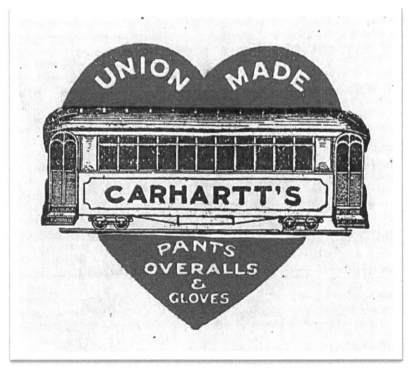

Early Carhartt trademark. Railcar over heart giving thanks to railroad workers.

Carhartt paid tribute to the railroad workers with one of his earliest logos: a heart overlaid with a railroad car to represent "Car" "Heart." The buttons on the overalls were a heart with the railroad car. Carhartt Inc. has global operations and depends heavily on American fabric and notions made in Georgia and Kentucky. Carhartt became the largest manufacturer in the world of work gloves and overalls. Carhartt showed the love in the brand name with the car-in-heart. The trademark is symbolic of how Hamilton Carhartt conducted his business and how he treated employees, buyers, and friends.

Carhartt work wear became a fashion trend in the 1980s and 1990s. Work wear became casual wear or street wear. Carhartt was challenged to keep up with demands as trendsetters appeared wearing the Carhartt brand. Actors and musicians make an ageless cool statement with the "Chunky Yellow C" Carhartt brand proudly visible. Who could have guessed that the world's best and most durable work clothes manufacturer would also become an iconic clothing manufacturer? The Carhartt Clothing brand continues to be the world's first choice in tough and comfortable work wear and now has a broad appeal in street wear and sportswear. Outdoor enthusiasts feel a bit smarter-sharper-snappier wearing the iconic Carhartt brand clothing.

Carhartt's advertisements showing his huge mill in Detroit included a statement at the bottom of the ad: Owner and sole proprietor of Hamilton Carhartt Cotton Mills, Rock Hill, SC, where the sweet Catawba flows and where the staple cotton grows.

Carhartt manufactured cars from 1910 to 1912.

Partial Timeline of Carhartt Clothing

Date	Timeline of Carhartt Clothing
1884	Hamilton Carhartt and Company, sold wholesale furniture.
1889	Founded Hamilton Carhartt and Company, manufacturing work clothing.
1905	Renamed Hamilton Carhartt Manufacturer Inc.
1907	Bought Rock Hill Cotton Factory in Rock Hill, South Carolina. Renamed to Hamilton Carhartt Cotton Mills.
1907-1909	Built Carhartt Plantation, Mansion, and Farm along Catawba River in Rock Hill.
1910	Renamed: Hamilton Carhartt Cotton Mills.
1910-1912	Carhartt Automobile Corporation was incorporated in 1910. Led by Hamilton Carhartt Jr. Closed 1912. Denim overalls were more profitable; total focus back to clothing.
1916-1917	Built Carhartt Cotton Mills Number 2 and the English Village in Rock Hill.
1937	Death of Hamilton and Annette Carhartt. His son, Wylie, became President.
1959	At the death of Wylie Carhartt, his son-in-law, Robert Charles Valade became President.
1965	After several name changes, Carhartt Inc. became the company's official corporate title.
1970s	Building of the Alaska Pipeline helped to grow the Carhartt brand.
1991	Carhartt work clothing began appearing in fashion shows in New York.

1993	Carhartt work clothing began appearing in <u>Vogue</u> and <u>Harper's Bazaar</u>.
1996	Mark Valade, great-grandson of Hamilton Carhartt Sr., became President. Gretchen Carhartt Valade, Mark's mother, became Board Chairman. Introduced flame-resistant garments.
1997	Introduced: a woman's line of clothing, babies and kids, and an extreme line for harsh weather conditions.
1998	Began manufacturing first-layer clothing: t-shirts and jeans.
2004	Formed partnership with Red Wing Shoe Company to provide professional-grade footwear to be sold under Carhartt brand.

The Carhartt Woodsman, Craft Beer
Carhartt partnered with New Holland Brewery in 2014
to create a beverage dedicated to Carhartt's customers.

Arnold Friedheim opened a store on Main Street in Rock Hill in 1866. The store offered a highly diversified stock of goods including Carhartt overalls. Lewis G. (Rabbit) Harris, an employee at Friedheim's store in the early 1900s, stated with pride that he sold the overalls, marked with a car superimposed on a heart, for about 60 years at Friedheim's in Rock Hill. Friedheim's store closed in 1965, which was a great loss for Rock Hill.

The Global Recession (1920-1921) preceding the 1929 Great Depression was brutal to the Carhartt Clothing Company along with other national/international manufacturers. The Company lost all its locations except plants in Atlanta, Detroit, and Dallas. They came close to shutting their doors for good. Surviving both drastic declines in manufactured goods speaks to the character, determination, and business genius displayed by Carhartt and his sons during that time. Despite the challenges of the Great Depression, Carhartt continued his strong commitment of employee benefits and support for workers' rights.

Hamilton Carhartt Sr., with his successful businessman's attitude, determination, and far-reaching vision, established a brand recognized worldwide as high-quality workers' clothing made with high-grade materials by proud and satisfied employees. Carhartt Inc. is still a privately held, family-owned company run by the descendants of founder Hamilton Carhartt Sr. with its headquarters in Dearborn, Michigan. They built and continue to maintain a solid reputation for quality clothing. Each generation has made the company stronger than ever while holding true to the values of the Founder.

The Carhartt Brand has stood the test of time.
Recognized for: Honesty, Trust, Satisfaction and Community.

CARHARTT COMPANY STANDARDS

"Set a standard of excellence, to which all others would aspire."
Hamilton Carhartt

It was a good day for Rock Hill when Hamilton Carhartt arrived. He created a more fair-minded and appealing Rock Hill. Hamilton Carhartt founded Carhartt Clothing with a dream to make the best denim and bib overalls while building a better life for his employees. He believed that "the prosperity of his employees created better denim." He lived his dream and lived his beliefs. The true wealth of Hamilton Carhartt was in his character.

Core Values as stated by Hamilton Carhartt:
- Honest value for an honest dollar.
- A square deal whether he works for me or buys from me.
- Set a standard of excellence, to which all others would aspire.
- Making good is merely a matter of exerting sufficient energy.
- If I can have but one thing, the respect of my customers or their business, I prefer the former, though I desire both, and trust I merit them.
- I believe that when I make a sale, I make a permanent friend.
- From the cotton boll to the overall. (He spun his own yarn, wove it on his own looms, and sewed it on his own machines.)
- I believe that when a man wears an article that I manufacture, his self-respect is increased because he knows that it is made by an honest manufacturer, who is honest with his employees.
- The most priceless ingredient of any product is the honesty and integrity of its maker.
- Merchandise that is honestly made to give service will create a lasting friendship.
- Our business was not started to do the gainful thing alone, but the just and honest thing, gainful if possible.
- The 'Carhartt Way' is to make denim better than any other. The prosperity of my employees creates better denim.
- The Attitude of a Successful Businessman: To spend 25 years in preparation, 25 years in application, and then, if successful, 25 years in recreation.
- My business of something over two million dollars annually, built up almost in a night, is not the result of any "gold brick" scheme, but of good honest values, first, last and all the time.
- We are building our business for the years, not for a season or two.
- The most valuable asset of the Carhartt Overall Company is its Good Will.
- If it carries the name Carhartt, its performance is legendary.

Slogans and Core Value Statements of Family and Company:

- Act Like Hamilton Carhartt: Be Inspired by Hardworking People.
- Respect Our Past While Walking Bravely into the Future.
- Today's Know-How with Yesterday's Integrity.
- My great-grandfather Ham once said, "Making good is merely a matter of exerting sufficient energy." Mark Valade referring to Hamilton Carhartt Sr.
- We believe Carhartt can help build a better future for everyone.

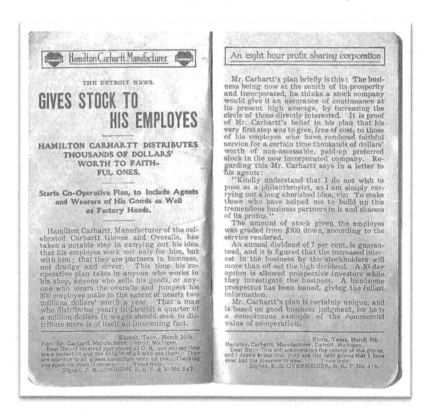

Hamilton Carhartt had a common touch and related to people of all ages and all levels of society. Area newspapers of that time gave statements from those who worked with Carhartt praising his character and how well he worked with his employees, his peers, and city and civic organizations. He believed in community and donated to local causes in Rock Hill as stated in these newspapers. He was an engaged citizen working with city leaders and other mill owners encouraging improvements in overall working and living conditions for employees. He worked with Winthrop College by giving financial resources and land toward providing kindergarten classes for the young. Carhartt's core values and company standards were his gifts to the future.

In the early days of the cotton mills, many farmers left their land to work in the cotton mills. Steady wages, a company store, and mill houses were strong attractions. In the South, early mill owners adopted a "parental role" toward their employees akin to the paternal manner that marked slave plantations. Mill owners provided basic housing with bare, basic living conditions—no indoor toilets, no running water nor electricity. Some medical services, schools, churches, and company stores were often in the villages. A strong bond developed among the people living in mill villages. Baseball teams were formed as well as other forms of social events. Early days for mill workers had many hardships including long hours, lack of safety, child labor, unhealthy conditions breathing dust and fluff, inadequate toilet facilities, and often a working environment with horrible conditions. Yards and streets were a muddy mess during wet weather.

Hamilton Carhartt took the basics to the best. While other mill workers worked 12 hours a day, Hamilton Carhartt started his business on an eight-hour schedule with union wages for workers. Upon employment, each employee became a stockholder earning 7% with the option to buy more stock. Living conditions were improved with inside toilets, hot and cold water, and electricity. Streets were graded and curbed with cement sidewalks, yards planted with grass, shrubbery, and flowers. He employed a nurse to care for the sick in the community and to see to the well-being of the children. He offered kindergarten and playgrounds for the children. He held regular outings and BBQs at his river-side mansion for his employees. His employees were 16 and older. In an advertisement in the Detroit Free Press, he mentions his reputation for big wages, sanitary working conditions, daylight work, restrooms, and laundries. In an interview with the Knoxville Sentinel, he stated the importance that he placed on hiring office boys because they would be his office managers in the years to come. He said that he wanted to give as many young men as possible a chance to make their way in the world. He ran his business with an active effort to help his employees build a better life. Carhartt left a legacy of care and concern for his employees, and he paved the way for his descendants to continue his legacy.

Carhartt's respect and concern for his employees is revealed in the work environment he provided for them. The Rock Hill, Fort Mill, and York newspapers and other public sources give accounts of the benefits enjoyed by Carhartt employees. Carhartt set the "Mill Parental Role Model" so high, it would be difficult for any other mill owner to reach.

Rock Hill, The Record, 10 July 1908
A barbeque event was held for employees of the Carhartt Mill on the Carhartt Farm. The event was a great success.

Rock Hill, The Record, 24 August 1909
Mr. Carhartt gave a picnic and barbeque for his employees and their families at his bungalow on the Catawba River.

COMMUNITY HOUSES at Carhartt Mills No. 1 and at No. 2:

- Community house at Mill No. 1 was a three-story building and faced the passenger depot on the corner of White and Wilson Streets. Community house at Mill No. 2 was in the center of the 30 artistic cottages. Community houses included: auditorium with stage, reading rooms, lecture rooms, kindergarten, nursery, sewing room, cooking room for classes, showers, tennis courts, billiard rooms, and first-aid rooms.
- Mill No. 1 had an indoor swimming pool for men and one for women. Indoor swimming pool at Carhartt Mill No. 2 was 40 by 80 feet.
- Gave employees opportunities to develop their talents. Provided equipment and instructors for a brass band for the men and a string orchestra for the women.
- Provided night schools with competent instructors available in all classes.
- Club houses held socials every Friday night for employees.

THE CHARIOT OF THE HAMILTON CARHARTT LADIES' BAND.
(This Ladies Band not in Rock Hill)

Carhartt Mills always had a waiting list of potential employees. Mr. Carhartt directed resources toward the general betterment of his employees. Mill workers tended to move from mill to mill hoping for higher wages and better working conditions. Workers in Carhartt's mills remained in place, taking advantage of the home living and working conditions provided and the opportunities for education for themselves and their children.

Charles A. Reese, a well-known and respected Rock Hill City Council member, and a long-time employee of the Rock Hill Evening Herald working in several areas including Assistant Publisher, had this to say about Mr. Carhartt: "Carhartt was a very friendly, heavy-set man, he would stop and talk to me when buying a paper. Carhartt was a striking sort of person."
(Charlie Reese was a young boy at that time selling papers.)

14

C. A. Drennan Sr., Rock Hill cotton grader and buyer,
"One of the finest men (Carhartt) I ever knew."

Robert M. (Bob) Ward is listed in the <u>Rock Hill City Directories</u> of 1936 and 1940-1941 as a reporter for the Herald Publishing Company. He states, "Mr. Carhartt was active in the civic life of Rock Hill and his influence was widely felt. He had an intense love of that place (Carhartt Plantation) far beyond the ordinary pride of possession. To him it was more than a quiet woodland home, it was his retreat."

Louise Pettus, tri-county historian, said that Carhartt cooperated with Mary Frayser and Winthrop College since 1913 by providing financial resources and donating mill property for childcare purposes, adult education, and recreational programs.

Gaffney, South Carolina, <u>The Gaffney Ledger</u>, 24 April 1920
Hamilton Carhartt Proffers Use of His Bungalow, Rock Hill, April 22.
Mr. Charles L. Cobb, of the People's National Bank of this city, today wired Congressman W. F. Stevenson the offer of Mr. Hamilton Carhartt's bungalow for President Wilson's use during the summer. The Carhartt bungalow, which is five miles north of Rock Hill and overlooking the Catawba River, would make a splendid place for the President's summer home. It is completely appointed and commands a beautiful view. Following is Mr. Cobb's telegram:

"Hon. W. F. Stevenson, care of House of Representatives, Washington, D.C.:
I have just received the following message from Hamilton Carhartt:
I wish to offer my home on the Catawba River, in the foothills of the Blue Ridge mountains, with its complete equipment of servants, Arabian saddle horses, automobiles, etc., to President Wilson for his Summer White House; it has ample accommodations for everybody, and I only hope he can see his way clear to accept it. Kindly put this matter before the proper authority. Will you be kind enough to extend Mr. Carhartt's invitation to President Wilson and assure the President that the people of South Carolina would be most happy to have him accept Mr. Carhartt's invitation and spend the summer months in our midst. Charles L. Cobb"

Louise Pettus states in the <u>York Enquirer</u> on 23 March 2003 that by 1920, Carhartt was spending most of his time on his model plantation on the Catawba River. That year, he sent the following telegram to President Woodrow Wilson: "I wish to offer my home on the Catawba River, in the foothills of the Blue Ridge Mountains, with its complete equipment of servants, Arabian saddle horses, automobiles, etc. to Pres. Wilson for his summer White House. It has ample accommodations for everybody." There was no reply.

Lynn Willoughby mentions in her book, <u>The "Good Town" Does Well: Rock Hill</u>, that Carhartt was active in the affairs and events in Rock Hill. He was one of the mill owners who encouraged other mill owners to provide for their employees: night schools, community centers, playgrounds for children, community garden space, and classes for women to learn new skills in household management.

Rock Hill, <u>The Record</u>, 17 June 1907, The Personality of the Man.
A banker in Detroit recently wrote to a gentleman in Rock Hill saying among other things: "Mr. Carhartt is a man of charming personality with the most beautiful manners, clearly marking him as a cultured man of the world. He is a prince in every sense of the word, full of the chivalry of the South and the ginger of the North."

Rock Hill, <u>The Record</u>, 19 September 1907
We are informed that the Carhartt Mill has installed a night school for the benefit of the operatives of its mill in this city.

Rock Hill, <u>The Record</u>, 22 March 1909
Mr. Hamilton Carhartt has given $50 to the Civic Improvement Club and $50 to the King's Daughters.

In 1982, Jane Clute interviewed Claude Huddleston, 79, for an article in <u>The Evening Herald</u> relating to working conditions in the Carhartt Mills. Mr. Huddleston told how convenient it was for mothers to nurse their babies while at work. Some mothers nursed their babies and the babies stayed at the mill all day. Women who had cooks would bring the baby to the mill, the mother would leave her job to feed the baby, and the cook would take the baby home. Women who lived close to the mill would walk home and care for the baby and return to work. Mr. Huddleston said, "All with management's blessing." In 1916, Mr. Huddleston "hired on" at Highland Park Mill when he was thirteen. He made seven cents an hour. Later that year in 1916, he went to work creeling warpers at Carhartt's Mill for $1.35 a day. "That was good money back then."

Rock Hill, The Record, 26 March 1917

Hamilton Carhartt offers new Mill and Village to Government.

Hamilton Carhartt has tendered to the Government the use of his Mill No. 2 and all buildings and cottages located at Carhartt on the Southern Railway for any purposes of the Government service in the war emergency, a most patriotic offer. This new mill has recently been organized with the same officers who direct Mill No. 1. Following is the letter making a tender of the property:

Honorable Newton D. Baker
Secretary of War
Washington, D.C.

My Dear Mr. Secretary:

For nearly a year, we have been building new buildings at Carhartt on the Southern Railway four miles north of this city, twenty miles south of Charlotte, North Carolina.

These buildings we have been expecting to use when completed for the second Hamilton Carhartt Cotton Mills and adjacent to these mills we are building something like thirty artistic cottages on the side hill for the accommodation of our employees.

These buildings, which are rapidly nearing completion, will all have every convenience of water, heat, light, and power and are most beautifully and delightfully situated at the foot of the Blue Ridge Mountains on the Catawba River.

Our president, who is with us now, wishes me to offer to you all these buildings for any purpose whatsoever that you may care to use them for either as a base hospital or for the manufacture of munitions or clothing or cloth for the same or indeed anything that you may choose.

Notwithstanding that the machinery and tools have been bought and paid for to fully equip the buildings as Cotton Mills. We will gladly defer doing this, if you care to take advantage of this offer for any use whatsoever.

I have the honor to be
Yours most respectfully,
W. G. Henderson
Treasurer and General Manager

Rock Hill, <u>The Record</u>, Monday, 11 March 1918
Liberal offer of Hamilton Carhartt to our Government
Offers His Plantation, and All it Contains, Free of All Cost
The following letter will be read with interest here:

Rock Hill, South Carolina
March 8, 1918

Dr. William C. Gorgas
Surgeon General, U.S.A.
Washington, D.C.

Dear Sir:
The writer owns about 1,400 acres of beautiful rolling land, located at Carhartt
Station on the Southern Railway, twenty miles south of Charlotte, N.C., and five
miles north of Rock Hill, S.C., a map of which is attached. This land extends for
three miles along the Catawba River in the foothills of the Blue Ridge Mountains.

Something like one-half of this property is under state of cultivation, and it has
splendid outbuildings, farmhouses, tenant houses, dairy barn, mule barn, cattle barn,
together with a herd of pure-blooded Guernsey cattle and seven saddle horses with
full equipment for riding.

The writer has his own temporary home, or lodge, on an eminence over-looking the
Catawba River. Nearby there is an extra cottage for visitors, and gardener's cottage.
All of these are in a splendid state of repair and furnished throughout completely.
Photographs enclosed.

The thought has occurred to me that Southern soldiers, invalided home from "over
there," would much prefer to recuperate in the Southern atmosphere and
environments, which are so dear to them, and I now propose to turn this entire
property, with all of its buildings and belongings, to the United States Government,
to be used as a hospital station, without any charge whatsoever for the same.

I will not only do this but will consider it a personal favor if you take this proposition
under consideration, and, if possible, accept the same and in addition, I hereby tender
you my personal service in any capacity that you can use me without any
compensation whatsoever. If you deem it worthwhile, I will come to Washington at
my own expense for an interview.

My own home, or lodge, can be used as headquarters for the officers and
superintendent of the place, and extra buildings can be put up very easily for hospital
wards, at locations that would be thought most desirable.

The plantation is well-supplied with water from an artesian well and from natural mineral springs, the waters of the latter having been analyzed and shown to be above reproach.

The buildings are all electric-lighted and there is an abundance of electric power furnished from an in-exhaustible supply from the Southern Power Company, one of whose great power stations is located nearby.

The land that is not under cultivation is heavily wooded with pine, cedar, juniper, maple, hickory, and other woods and are intersected with foot and bridle paths throughout and all in all it seems to me that this would make a more desirable location for a hospital unit.

The writer also owns 2 cotton mills in the near vicinity of this property and if any of the maimed or crippled soldiers wanted to have employment, we would go out of our way to see that it was given them and we would freely give of our time and money to see that they were properly trained in the vocation of the cotton industry.

Trusting you will see and appreciate this offer, and that I may have the courtesy of an acknowledgment at your convenience, I am,

Yours very truly,
Hamilton Carhartt

In times of international conflict, Carhartt committed to "backing the attack." The company offered seven Carhartt facilities to the government for the purpose of creating uniforms for the U.S. military in World War I.

During World War II, the company made coveralls for soldiers and support personnel, jungle suits for Marines in the Pacific, and workwear for women entering the workforce in American factories. Carhartt was one of the world's largest suppliers of military wear.

September 11, 2001: Carhartt Clothing Company donated thousands of bib overalls to the rescue workers at the World Trade Center.

Covid-19 Pandemic, 2020 and Ongoing: Carhartt Clothing Company joined the preventive effort to reduce the chances of infection by making protective masks and medical gloves. During the pandemic, Carhartt donated over $300,000 to help students find career paths in skilled trades.

During World War I, Carhartt sent shipments of small-sized overalls to Europe to help clothe the orphans created by the war. He received a letter of appreciation from the Committee for the Protection of European Children.

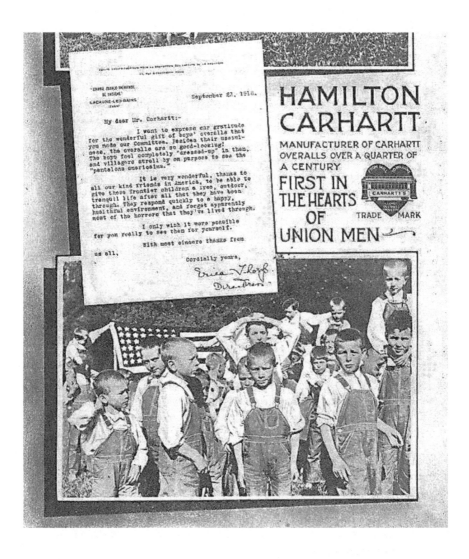

Hamilton Carhartt's relationship with his employees was noted in a monthly employee newsletter created to show his appreciation to his employees. He wrote poetry for this publication. In this poem, he is encouraging his employees to contribute and to become a part of the employee newsletter.

Hand Clasps Across Space
by Hamilton Carhartt

SEND IT IN
If you have a bit of news
Send it in
Or a joke that will amuse
Send it in
A story that is true
An incident that's new
I want to hear from you
Send it in
Never mind about the style
If the news is worth the while
It may help or cause a smile
Send it in

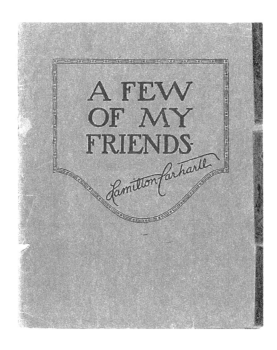

Carhartt's love of Rock Hill, the Catawba River, and natural beauty is shown in the small booklet written by him and entitled The Carhartt Plantation.

I'm hungerin' to get away
Down yonder where the catfish play,
Down yonder where the skies are blue;
And every breeze that blows is true.

Walking along the Catawba River
So peaceful in its flow,
Where the hills stand out forever
Quiet hills that thrill one so.
You who stand upon the brim
of the Catawba with history old.

Knoxville, Tennessee, Knoxville Sentinel, 20 April 1921, page 7
Runs Big Business on Sentiment
From a peddler of pants to "Overall King" in 30 years. That is the record of Hamilton Carhartt of York, S.C. who has built a pretty hunting lodge known as "The Plantation" on his beautiful 1600 acres estate at Carhartt's Station on Catawba River in York County near one of his big overall mills. There he raises Arabian horses, Shetland ponies, Corneaux pigeons and Rhode Island Red chickens and hooks fish in the tawney Catawba. He is "self-made."

Born in Jackson, Michigan, in 1860, as a young man he never seemed to get ahead. In 1886 he was selling pants and other clothing over the northwest from a prairie schooner. He had calls for a work garment. He could not supply them. Why not manufacture it. He was without capital, but he raised enough money to buy two sewing machines and a little cloth. The little business grew and prospered. There are big factories now bearing his name in Detroit, Atlanta, Dallas, San Francisco, Toronto, Rock Hill, SC, Carhartt, South Carolina, Elberton, Georgia and Mobile, Alabama.

"My ambition, he says, is to run the business successfully and to give a great many young men a chance to make their way in the world. My associates in the business are my closest friends, my chums. If it weren't for the fun there is in working with them and being with them, I wouldn't—I couldn't stay in business. I run my business on sentiment. If I didn't, it would not be successful, and it wouldn't be worth running. What makes an organization successful? Isn't it the loyalty and the enthusiasm of the many men engaged in it? And how can any man inspire these sentiments if he has no sentiment in his own makeup? No one man can run a big concern; he must depend upon others for the actual doing of everything. To get the right kind of men, we begin early. We are more particular about the hiring of office boys than about any other thing connected with the Carhartt company. The office boys of today will be our office managers of tomorrow."

Carhartt built his reputation by using top quality in everything that he did. His family has followed his example and maintained the reputation of the best manufacturer of outdoor work clothing in the world. In recent years, his clothing brand has become iconic for sportswear and street wear.

Carhartt's work clothes and Arabian horses were listed nationally and internationally with the address of Rock Hill, South Carolina. He placed Rock Hill on the World Map.

Some things never change:
Love, hope, morals, courtesy,
and Carhartt Company Standards.

Today's know-how with Yesterday's Integrity.
No tweaking needed.

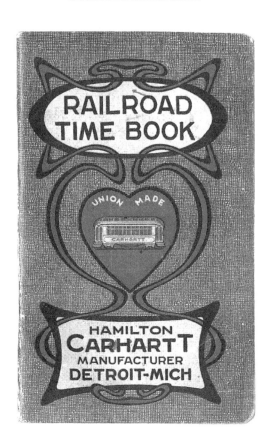

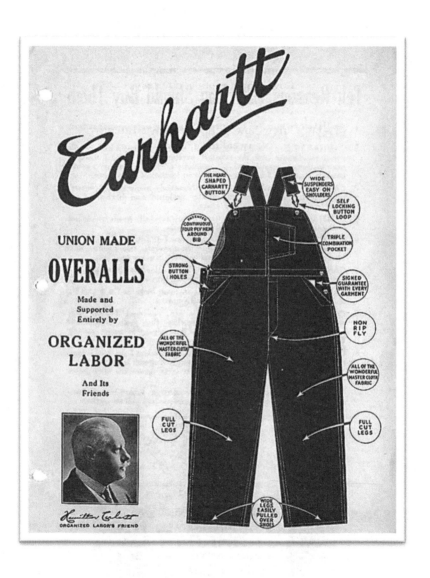

HAMILTON CARHARTT COTTON MILLS IN ROCK HILL

"I believe that when I make a sale, I make a permanent friend."
Hamilton Carhartt

HAMILTON CARHARTT COTTON MILLS. ROCK HILL. S. C.

Hamilton Carhartt Cotton Mills No. 1, Rock Hill
Postcard Courtesy of Stephen Turner

Hamilton Carhartt Cotton Mills No. 1, 1907 - 1925
Corner of Chatham Avenue and White Street
Rock Hill, South Carolina

Several Confederate veterans including James M. Ivy, Adolphus Eugene Hutchison, Andrew Hutchison White, and others began textile manufacturing in 1881 in Rock Hill with the Rock Hill Cotton Factory. Mill owners in the tri-county area of York, Chester, and Lancaster Counties built villages around their mills which included housing, schools, churches, and stores. Mill villages were self-contained. Housing was provided within walking distance of the mill as transportation was rare. Rock Hill and the tri-county area began changing from an agricultural environment to textile manufacturing in the early 1880s.

Predating the birth of the railroad and Rock Hill, the White Family and the Black Family owned the land in what became downtown Rock Hill. The Black Family owned what became Main Street/Black Street and beyond. The White Family owned what became White Street and beyond. The Main Street-White Street meeting of land was called the "Black and White Line."

The Rock Hill Cotton Factory bought most of their land from Anne Hutchison White (1805-1880). Anne married George Pendleton White (1801-1849), grandson of Thomas "Kanawha" Spratt. George caught pneumonia while supervising his railroad line building crew and passed away leaving Anne to raise four children and take care of the farm. Anne was the daughter of David Hutchison, one of the earliest settlers to lease land from the Catawba Indians. Anne is known as the "Mother of Rock Hill." She used her inheritance from her husband and from her brother, Hiram Hutchison, to provide land for the first school in Rock Hill, pay off the debt on First Presbyterian Church on Main Street, and to continually enlarge and improve the White Home. Each generation of the Hutchison Family has continued to give their time and resources toward the betterment of Rock Hill. Andrew Hutchison White (1843-1903) and William Campbell Hutchison (1858-1931) both served as mayors of Rock Hill. The White Home was listed on the National Register of Historic Places in 1969 and is now owned and operated by Historic Rock Hill as a history museum and meeting place for special events.

The Rock Hill Cotton Factory, now known as the Cotton Factory at the corner of Chatham and White Streets, is dear to Rock Hillians, as it represents the foundation of Rock Hill and the move from agriculture to industry. Rock Hill grew from the cotton industry, the railroad, and the cotton mills. Many business leaders, including Hamilton Carhartt, kept this mill active. Thanks to Williams & Fudge Inc. for preserving this landmark for the people.

Cotton Factory Plaza as restored by Williams & Fudge Inc.

Early Cotton Mills in Rock Hill

Date	Cotton Factory
1880-1881	Rock Hill Cotton Factory First Cotton Mill in Rock Hill First Steam-Powered Mill in the South
1888/1889	Standard - Highland Park
1890	Globe - Victoria (Demolished)
1896	Arcade
1896	Manchester - Blue Buckle - Industrial
1907	Aragon - Aragon Baldwin
1907/1909	Wymojo (Wylie/Moore/Johnson) (Demolished)
1929	RH Printing & Finishing (Bleachery)
1948	Celanese (Celriver)
1940s	Dave R. Baer Hosiery Mill Samarkand Rugs Inc.
1959	Bowater - New-Indy Containerboard

The path from the Rock Hill Cotton Factory to Hamilton Carhartt Cotton Mill No. 1 travels through bankruptcies and many name changes. Records indicate this path: Rock Hill Cotton Factory, Belvedere Mill, Crescent Cotton Mill, Chicora Cotton Mill, Bellevue Mill, and Hamilton Carhartt Cotton Mills in 1907.

A Notice of Bankrupt Sale appeared in The Evening Herald, 19 July 1905. Southern Textile Company, formerly Rock Hill Cotton Factory and Chicora Mill, was listed for sale to highest bidder on: Tuesday, 25th July 1905, 2:00 p.m. The cotton mill property including the buildings, machinery and about eight acres of land and twenty-four tenement houses . . .

York County Government Center
Congress Street, York, South Carolina
<u>Register of Deeds</u>

    1905   Book 25, pages 398-405, 8 Acres and other
                 Southern Textile Company, declared Bankruptcy
                 16 November 1904,
                 sold to
                 International Trust Company of Maryland
                 Walter Coles Cabell appointed Trustee of
                          Southern Textile Company
                 Sale held 25 July 1905, 3 parcels, $110,500
                 Property known as Chicora. Deed dated 4 September 1903
                 advertised in Rock Hill Herald as Chicora Mill
                 Recorded: December 4, 1905

    1905   Book 25, pages 531-534, 28 December, 8 Acres Rock Hill
                 International Trust Company of Maryland
                 sold to Bellevue Mills of New Jersey, 3 parcels, $325,000
                 Recorded: January 12, 1906

    1907   Book 27, page 492, 8 Acres, Rock Hill
                 Bellevue Mills Company
                 sold to Hamilton Carhartt
                 Recorded: May 13, 1907

Bellevue Mills Company sold to Hamilton Carhartt Cotton Mills:

This Indenture made this first day of May A.D. 1907, between the Bellevue Mills Company, a corporation organized and existing under the laws of the State of New Jersey, party of the first part, and the Hamilton Carhartt Cotton Mills, a corporation organized and existing under the laws of the State of New York, party of the second part.

Witnesseth: That the said party of the first part, for and in consideration of the sum of Ten ($10) dollars, to in hand paid by the party of the second part the receipt whereof is hereby acknowledged, hath granted, bargained sold and conveyed and by these presents doth grant, bargain sell and convey unto the said party of the second part.

All that certain lot and parcel of land, with the buildings thereon erected, together with the machinery appliances and supplies, contained in the same, situated in the County of York, in the State of South Carolina, and in the city of Rock Hill, on the Northwest side of the track of the Southern Railway Company beginning at a stake at the corner of White and Wilson streets inside of the pavement and running thence said Wilson Street north forty nine (49) degrees east five hundred and forty-five (545) feet to a stake twelve (12) feet from the center of the main track of the South Carolina and Georgia Extension Railroad Company thence parallel with said railroad track twelve (12) feet from center of same a distance of eight hundred and seventy two (872) feet to a stake sixty five (65) feet from the center of the Southern Railway Company's track, thence by a line parallel with the track of the said Southern Railway Company's track sixty five feet from the center thereof a distance of fifty five (55) and one half degrees west one hundred and twenty two (122) feet to a stake at the corner of the Southern Railway's lot thence south forty seven and one half (47 ½) degrees west four hundred (400) feet to a stake at the corner of Chatham and White streets inside of the pavement thence north thirty-eight (38) degrees west three hundred and twenty seven (327) feet to the stake at the corner of Commercial Warehouse lot thence with line of said lot north forty six and one half (46 ½) degrees east one hundred and thirty four (134) feet to the center of trailway side track, thence north thirty eight (38) degrees west one hundred and forty two (142) feet to a stake, thence south fifty two (52) degrees west one hundred and thirty two and one half (132 ½) feet to a stake on White Street inside of pavement, thence north thirty eight (38) degrees west two hundred and eighty five (285) feet to the beginning, containing eight and seven tenths (8 7/10) acres, more or less bounded by the South Carolina and Georgia Extension Railroad Company's main track by the Southern Railway's track by Chatham, White and Wilson Streets and by the Commercial Warehouse lots, being property known as the Chicora Cotton Mills. Together with all and singular the rights, members hereditaments and appurtenances to the said premises belonging or in anywise incident or appertaining thereto.

To have and to hold the above described premises and all the privileges and appurtenance thereto belonging, to the said party of the second part, its successors and assigns forever, to its only use and behoof; and the said party of the first part covenants with the party of the second part that it will warrant and forever defend the title to the same to the party of the second part and the successors and assigns of the alinee under it, from and against the right title or claim of it and it successors, both at law and in equity, and against every other person whomsoever, claiming, or to claim the same or any part thereof.

In Testimony whereof, the said Bellevue Mills Company has caused these presents to be signed by its President and its corporate seal to be hereunto affixed, attested by its secretary the day and year first above written.

Signed sealed and delivered in the presence of
Joseph Del Junker and Henry M. Earle

> Bellevue Mills Company (Seal)
> by Peter H. Coor Vice-President
> Attest: T. Ashby Blythe, Secretary

State of New York, City of New York
Personally appeared before me Joseph Del Junker and made oath that he saw the corporate seal of the Bellevue Mills company affixed to the above written deed; and that he also saw T. Ashby Blythe, Secretary of said Bellevue Mills Company sign and attest the same, and that he also saw Peter H. Coor, Vice-President of the Bellevue Mills Company sign the same and that said deponent with Henry M. Earle witnessed the execution and delivery thereof as the act and deed of said Bellevue Mills Company.

Joseph Del Junker
Subscribed and sworn to before me this first day of May A.D. 1907
Witness by hand and notarial seal
Lewis Earle (Seal)
Notary Public New York Co.
My commission expires March 30, 1908

State of New York
I, Peter J. Dooling Clerk of the county of New York and also clerk of the Supreme Court for the said county the same being a court of record, do hereby certify that Lewis Earle before whom the annexed deposition was taken, was at the time of taking the same a Notary Public of New York dwelling in said county, duly appointed and sworn and authorized to administer oaths to be used in any court in said State, and for general purposes, that I am well acquainted with the handwriting of said Notary and that his signature thereto is genuine as I verily believe.

In testimony whereof I have hereunto set my hand and affixed the seal of the said court the 8th day of May 1907.
    Peter J. Dooling, Clerk (Seal) Recorded May 13, 1907

Hamilton Carhartt renamed the Bellevue Mill to Hamilton Carhartt Cotton Mills. Within a few years, Rock Hill was known worldwide for the production of denim overalls.

Child Labor Laws and Compulsory Education Laws were hard won in the United States. Some mills relied heavily on child labor and other mill owners did not. Hamilton Carhartt started manufacturing apparel for working men in 1889 in Detroit on an eight-hour a day schedule with union wages. His advertisements were for workers 16 years old and older.

Ad from the Detroit Free Press on 22 September 1918
    GIRLS 16 TO 19 YEARS LEARN A TRADE
    25 vacancies open, making Carhartt overalls.
    A worth-while guaranteed weekly wage while learning.
    Competent instructors—speaking any language.
    You know CARHARTT reputation for big wages,
    sanitary conditions, a daylight factory, restrooms, laundries, etc.
    Just let us show you. Ask for Miss Gendron.
    HAMILTON CARHARTT COTTON MILLS,
    Michigan Ave. between 10th and 11th Sts.

By 1903, South Carolina passed Child Labor Legislation stating that no child under 10 could work in a factory and by 1905, no child under 12. Though not routinely enforced, child labor in the South began to dwindle. Compulsory Education Laws were passed in an effort to remove children from the factories and also to eliminate illiteracy. By 1918, all of the United States had Compulsory Educations Laws though enforcement was not immediately effective.

Carhartt Archives: Hamilton Carhartt & Company, Detroit, Mich., 1900

Paragraph from booklet written by Hamilton Carhartt:
It can hardly come within the province of the church to assume the role of regulator of business affairs. But that it can exert a powerful moral influence in the amelioration of the relations between employer and employee will not be questioned. The movement thus so practically inaugurated suggests to the churches a line of effort to which public sentiment may be so aroused concerning the wrongs which underpaid labor is undergoing, not only in England but in many cities and communities of our own land, that a much-needed reform will be the result.
                                        Very respectfully, Hamilton Carhartt & Company

Rock Hill, The Record, 31 January 1907
Mr. Carhart [sic] of Detroit was in the city with parties who are interested in the Belleview Mills. He needs cloth for manufacturing overalls.

Rock Hill, The Record, 7 February 1907
The Syleecau Manufacturing Company, J. C. Cauthen manager, has purchased the 250-horsepower steam engine formerly used by the Belleview Mills, which has been replaced by electrical equipment. The old engine will be broken up and sold for scrap.

Rock Hill, The Record, 15 April 1907
Mr. R. A. Blythe, Col. Peter Caw, Col. Carheart [sic]. Mr. Mackey, and Mr. W. H. Harris, president of Bellevue Mills, were in Rock Hill. They may consider expanding the Bellevue Mills. Mr. Carheart is hunting for a mill that can supply materials for his overalls' factories.

Rock Hill, The Record, 22 April 1907

"Carhartt Buys Bellevue Mills." The Record quotes a report from the Textile Manufacturer's Journal that Hamilton Carhartt Cotton Mills was incorporated under New York laws with a capital of $500,000. This company has purchased the mills formerly known as Chicora Mills in Rock Hill, S. C. They will take possession on May 1st. This plant is one of the mills incorporated in the Southern Textile Company and subsequently purchased by the Belleview (sic) Cotton Mills. It is stated that the plant will be doubled in size and a dye house added. The output will be denim and will be used by Hamilton Carhartt, manufacturer of overalls, Detroit, Mich. This concern is one of the largest overalls manufacturers in the country and consumes a large product annually.

Rock Hill, The Record, 27 June 1907

Extensive improvements will be made to the houses occupied by the operatives of the Carhartt Mill. The houses will be modernized, and electric lights will be added. A new street parallel with the railroad on the north side of the mill has been laid out and a number of handsome cottages erected on the same. Manager Adams has told The Record that the company has contracted to lay cement pavements all though the mill village. Improvements at the mill: the boilers have been removed and a dye room placed in that location, and they are erecting a transformer house at the rear of the mill.

Mr. Carhartt took possession of the mill on 1 May 1907. He added his name to the building in November 1907. "Glacial pace" was not a part of his character. He immediately began building and improving. Rock Hill contractors, Love and Owens (Franklin Sadler Love and Frank Owens), built a three-story addition on to the now Hamilton Carhartt Cotton Mills. Mr. Biberstein of Charlotte was the architect and Capt. A. D. Holler supervised the construction. Mr. Holler built most of the mills in Rock Hill as well as the still-occupied Anderson House at 227 Oakland Avenue, Rock Hill, built in 1898. The Carhartt mill was converted from steam to electricity about 1907. Converting from steam to electrical power reduced the annual power cost about half for most mills. Dyeing equipment, cutting machines, and sewing machines were added about 1909 to make bib overalls. Prior to the sewing machines added at Carhartt Mill No. 1, denim was sent to his Detroit Mill to be sewn into overalls. His slogan was "from the cotton boll to the overall."

Hamilton Carhartt Cotton Mill No. 1. Name appears in upper right.
Photo Courtesy of Gary Williams

Carhartt advertising his cotton mills in Rock Hill:
Mr. Carhartt has recently issued a handsomely printed booklet as "a testimonial to his friends of the Switchmen's Union of North America and his companions in industry." This little book contains a description of the river and lake outings he gives his employees and their families.

Hamilton Carhartt used the upper floor of the house on the right as his residence, until the mansion was completed on Carhartt Plantation.
Lower floor was office for the mill.
Postcard Courtesy of Robert Ratterree

33

Rock Hill, The Record, 6 January 1908

The office force of the Carhartt Mills has moved into their elegant new quarters, in the two-story building erected on the corner adjoining the plant, and now have the handsomest office quarters in the city, and one of the best in the state. The furniture is of the handsomest mahogany being solid and very beautiful. The upper story is being fitted up for living quarters, Mr. Carhartt intends to inhabit them when in the city. There is a dining room and cook room on the first floor, and sleeping apartments, etc. and which will be very convenient and comfortable quarters. Men are now fencing the property.

Building on right was office for Hamilton Carhartt Cotton Mills No. 1
Postcard Courtesy of Robert Ratterree

Rock Hill, The Record, 10 January 1908

There was a small blaze at the Carhartt Mills Thursday morning, but the sprinkler system worked and extinguished the flames.

Rock Hill, The Record, 15 February 1909

Mr. Carhartt will let contracts for work on the mill in Rock Hill. Work will include a new front to the mill (140 feet by 35 feet), a new monitor on the mill, a 4 ½ foot betterment wall around the entire building and sixteen new tenement houses to be erected on the property in front of the Rock Hill Buggy Company on land he recently purchased for $8,000.

Rock Hill, <u>The Record</u>, 18 March 1909

Mr. Hamilton Carhartt was in the city this week. At his mill, they are now moving dirt and preparing for laying the foundation of a new weave room, to be 140 feet by 140 feet to accommodate about one hundred looms. Work on the building will begin Monday. Mr. Biberstein of Charlotte is architect and Capt. A. D. Holler will supervise the construction. The new building will extend from the main building down to White Street, in front of the roller mill and as soon as completed they will move all of the looms from the main building to this building and install other machinery in the main building.

1917 Local National Guard Troops boarding for WWI deployment.
Hamilton Carhartt Mill visible above train depot roof.
Photo Courtesy of Chip Hutchison and Totty Wilkerson

Rock Hill, <u>The Record</u>, 17 November 1919
TO ENLARGE MILL VILLAGE

The mill village of Hamilton Carhartt Cotton Mill in this city will be greatly extended to meet the requirements of the new mill addition. The village layout and engineering work is being done by plans of E. S. Draper, landscape architect and city planner, Charlotte, and New York City. N. G. Walker of Rock Hill is architect of houses and structures.

Rock Hill, <u>The Record</u>, 27 March 1913
Love & Owens were awarded another contract yesterday by Hamilton Carhartt to add another story to the addition now being built to the Carhartt mill property, which is to provide more room for the manufacture of overalls. The first contract to Love & Owens called for one additional story only. When the job is completed, it will make quite a showing.

<u>Mill News</u>, The Great Southern Weekly for Textile Workers
Vol. XXII, No. 16, October 14, 1920
Hamilton Carhartt Company, Carhartt, South Carolina, has adopted our system of Dustless Card Stripping and Broomless Flow Sweeper for all of his mills.

Here are a few land transactions of the Rock Hill Cotton Factory representing the bumpy road traveled to become today's heart of history in Knowledge Park.

York County Government Center, Register of Deeds

Date	Register of Deeds
1880	Rock Hill Cotton Factory began buying land: (List not complete) Book B-2, page 791, 5 Acres, Rock Hill from A. H. White et al. Book C-3, page 320, Lot Rock Hill from A. H. White et al. Book C-3, page 466, 7.5 Acres Rock Hill from G. E. M. Steele Book F-7, page 761, Lot Rock Hill from John Ratterree Book H-9, page 562, Lot Rock Hill from Jas. S. White et al. Book J-10, page 133, Lot Rock Hill from W. B. Fewell
1880	Incorporated by the state of South Carolina in March 1880 Construction on Mill began in April
1881	Mill began operation in May. Adolphus Eugene Hutchison, president
1898	Reorganized and Renamed Belvedere Mills W. C. Hutchison, President (William Campbell Hutchison, son of original president served as Rock Hill Mayor 1896-1898)
1898	Book 18, Page 52, May 19 Rock Hill Cotton Factory sold to Kate J. Hutchison 378 acres in Blackjacks on Taylor Creek for $1,200. A. E. Hutchison President, D. Hutchison, Treasurer Recorded: October 5, 1898 Mill idle, ceased operation in July

1899	Book 19, pages 186-187 R. Lee Kerr, Receiver, appointed 17 January 1899 sold to Dr. J. H. McAden Public Auction on 7 June 1899, no offers, 26 July 1899 second auction Sold to Dr. J. H. McAden of Charlotte, only bid, $31,000 Entire property of Rock Hill Cotton Factory Renamed Crescent Cotton Mills of Rock Hill Recorded: January 4, 1900 Book 18, pages 695-697 Charter: Crescent Cotton Mills Recorded: August 14, 1899
1900	Book 19, page 370, 6 Acres, Rock Hill Crescent Cotton Mill sold to James M. Cherry and J. G. Anderson Recorded: February 24, 1900 Book 19, pages 756-757 John H. McAden, Mecklenburg County, North Carolina sold to Crescent Cotton Mills $36,000 paid by Crescent Cotton Mills. Formerly belonged to Rock Hill Cotton Factory Company and deeded me by R. Lee Kerr, Receiver of the Rock Hill Cotton Factory on (undated) 1899 Recorded: August 9, 1900
1901	Book 20, page 512, 30th August 1900 Crescent Cotton Mill, Isaac S. Cohen Trustee A. E. Smith Receiver of Crescent Cotton Mill to Isaac S. Cohen Trustee Samuel Friedheim W. B. Fewell afterwards became a party corporation to be insolvent Published in The Herald 11 February 1901 Recorded: February 22, 1901 Book 20, pages 548-550, February 11 Isaac S. Cohen, Trustee to Chicora Cotton Mills Bought by me, Isaac Cohen, for the stockholders of Chicora Cotton Mills paid by Chicora Cotton Mills $34,000 A. E. Smith receiver, Samuel Friedheim the Crescent Cotton Mills Recorded: March 4, 1901 Book 20, page 560, Charter M. R. Cooper, Secretary of State sold to Chicora Cotton Mills Recorded: March 8, 1901

1903	Book 23, page 168, 8 Acres, Rock Hill Chicora Cotton Mills sold to Southern Textile Company For $1 and other valuable considerations J. S. Cohen, President Recorded: September 14, 1903
1905	Rock Hill, <u>The Evening Herald</u>, July 19 Notice of Sale In the matter of the Southern Textile Company, Bankrupt. Sale: Tuesday, 25th July 1905, 2:00 p.m. to highest bidder the cotton mill property known as the Chicora Mill, including the buildings and machinery situated thereon at Rock Hill, County of York, State of South Carolina. Consisting of about eight acres of land upon which are erected the mill building and twenty-four tenement houses . . .
1905	Book 25, pages 398-405, 8 Acres and other Southern Textile Company, declared Bankruptcy November 16, 1904 sold to International Trust Company of Maryland Walter Coles Cabell appointed Trustee of Southern Textile Co. Sale held 25 July 1905, 3 parcels, $110,500 Property known as Chicora. Deed dated September 4, 1903, advertised in Rock Hill <u>Herald</u> as Chicora Mill Recorded: December 4, 1905 Book 25, pages 531-534, 28 December, 8 Acres Rock Hill International Trust Company of Maryland sold to Bellevue Mills of New Jersey, 3 parcels $325,000 Recorded: January 12, 1906
1907	Book 27, page 492, 8 Acres, Rock Hill Bellevue Mills Company sold to Hamilton Carhartt Recorded: May 13, 1907
1921	Mill closed during the Global Recession of 1920-1921 following World War I. The Global Recession created a drop in manufacturing production forcing many plants to close in both America and Europe.
1925	Book 65, pages 413-415 Carhartt Overall Company sold to Cutter Cotton Mfg. Company Carhartt Overall Company -Wylie W. Carhartt, Vice-President Recorded: August 8, 1928

1946	John. H. Cutter sold mill to M. C. Goldberg of Philadelphia Renamed Gold-Tex Fabrics Corporation 1948, William Thomas succeeded Mr. Paul as resident manager 1949, Robert A. Morgan succeeded Mr. Thomas as resident manager
1963	Closed: Economic Recession
1965	Sold to Sol Aberman and Edward Aberman Renamed Edwards Mills
1966?	Plat Book 29, page 131 (no date listed on page) Reserved sheet but never recorded Property of Sol and Bessie Aberman
1967	Closed and listed For Sale
1968	Bought by Ostrow Textile Company Renamed Plej's Textile Mill Outlet
1992	Listed on National Register of Historic Places
2000	Closed
2001	Acquired by the Rock Hill Economic Development Corporation
2006	Bought by Williams & Fudge Inc. renovated into offices Renamed Cotton Factory Plaza (Williams & Fudge Inc. business began 18 July 1986)
2007	Historical Marker 46-38 erected at West White Street and Chatham Avenue by the Culture and Heritage Museums of York County and the City of Rock Hill in conjunction with Williams & Fudge Inc.

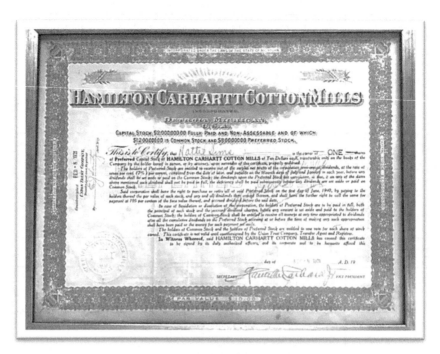

February 8, 1921
Photo Courtesy of Gary Williams

Button used on Carhartt Overalls
showing appreciation to railroad workers.

One of the four Carhartt Cotton Mills in the South but not Rock Hill
Carhartt Archives: Hamilton Carhartt & Company, Detroit, Mich., 1900

Paragraphs from booklet written by Hamilton Carhartt:
The question has often been asked us, as to what do we attribute our great success in the manufacturing business. Commencing, as we did a few years ago with absolutely nothing, while today we are pressing for first place, firms that have grown gray in the business, and have ten, yes, twenty times the capital that we have, our answer has invariably been that we have reasons three:

> First: We have always been thoroughly in love with our business.
> Second: We have always made honest goods.
> Third: We have always been honest with our employees.

Now, to be thoroughly in love with our business means that our trade of manufacturing working clothes of all descriptions for men has our whole and undivided attention, backed by the inspiration that by making the goods, and these only, in a perfect and wear-resisting manner, we are not only winning success for ourselves, but are doing a Christian act to the men who toil, who wear our garments.

In all speculations man has been tacitly figured as a clothed animal, when he is by nature a naked animal and, next to the loaf of bread to sustain life, the most essential thing to him is the where-with-all to cover his carcass. To supply this covering in a way that shall leave nothing to be desired we have made a life's study.

41

Hamilton Carhartt Cotton Mills No. 2, 1916/1917-1925

Carhartt Station, Carhartt, South Carolina
(Now: Celriver Road/Red River Road)

Hamilton Carhartt Cotton Mills No. 2
Staff Photo, The Evening Herald

Hamilton Carhartt's mill in Rock Hill was doing well. He was actively involved with other mill owners, working with Winthrop College by donating resources to help with kindergarten age as well as future-teacher training for young women, working with city leaders to encourage improvements for mill villages, and reaching out to local groups with financial resources who were involved in helping the needy. Articles show that he was deeply impressed with the geographical location of Rock Hill. He began to expand his holdings to include building a second mill and a plantation that became known statewide for progressive agriculture and the introduction of new breeding animals including Arabian horses. He created a second home for his family in Rock Hill.

Fort Mill Times, 10 August 1916
CARHARTT MILL A CERTAINTY
According to the Rock Hill Record, there is no longer any doubt of the purpose of Hamilton Carhartt to erect a cotton mill at Carhartt, three miles south of Fort Mill. The village at present will contain 30 houses, laid out in circular plan, a community house in the center. The mill will be built of rubble stone foundation and piers, with brick panels, all openings to have large steel section sash. The building will be the most modern of its kind in the Carolinas. All the houses in the village will be of individual design and pebble dash outside. A complete water, sewerage and electric lighting system will be installed

York County Government Center
Congress Street, York, South Carolina
<u>Register of Deeds</u>
Book 44, page 813
Hamilton Carhartt Mill #2

Charter

The State of South Carolina
Executive Department, By the Secretary of State

Whereas, Hamilton Carhartt of Carhartt, S.C., and H. G. Henderson, of Rock Hill, S. C., did on the 20th of Oct. 1916, file with the Secretary of State a written Declaration, signed by themselves, setting forth:

FIRST: The names-residences of said petitioners to be as given as above.

SECOND: The name of the proposed corporation be that of
                Hamilton Carhartt Cotton Mills No. 2

THIRD: The principal place of business of the corporation will be at
                Carhartt, S.C.

FOURTH: The general purpose of the corporation and the nature of business
                it proposes to do is to manufacture cotton into yard (sic)
                and cloth and conduct a general cotton manufacturing
                establishment; to gin cotton, and to manufacture cotton seed into
                its products.

FIFTH: The amount of the capital stock to be Five Hundred Thousand
                Dollars (three hundred thousand common stock and two hundred
                thousand 7% cumulative Preferred stock), and the number of
                shares into which the same is to be divided to be five thousand,
                of the par value of One Hundred dollars each.

SIXTH: The capital stock to be payable as set forth in the Declaration and
                Petition.

AND WHEREAS, on 20th day of October 1916 the date above named petitioners were commissioned by me as a Board of Corporations:

AND WHEREAS, the said Board of Corporators, on the eighth day of Jan. 1917 did file with the Secretary of State, their return in writing, over their signatures, certifying, among other things, that pursuant to published notice as required in the commission of the said Corporators, the books of subscription to the capital stock of the aforesaid company were duly opened, and that there upon exceeding fifty per cent of the capital stock was subscribed by bona fide stock holders, that thereupon a meeting of stockholders was called, and the aforesaid company was duly organized and by the election of a Board of Directors, and other necessary officers. That

44

furthermore, they have complied with all the requirements of the Code of Laws of the State of South Carolina of 1912, and all Acts or parts of Acts amendatory thereto. NOW THEREFORE, I, R. M. McCowan, Secretary of State, by virtue of the authority in me vested by the aforesaid Code and Acts amendatory thereto do hereby certify that the said Company has been fully organized according to the laws of South Carolina under the name and for the purpose indicated in their written declaration and that they are fully authorized to commence business under their charter, and I do hereby direct that a copy or this certificate be filed and recorded in the office of the Register of Mesne (sic) Conveyance in each county where such Corporation shall have a business office.

Given under my hand and seal of the State, at Columbia this Eighth Day of January 1916, in the year of our Lord one thousand nine Hundred and seven and in the one hundred and forty first year of the Independence of the United States of America.

(Seal)   R. M. McCowan
         Secretary of State

Recorded this the 29th day of June 1920.

Added Handwritten Note:
Pursuant to law the capital stock of the within corporation has on this day increased to the sum of $1,000,000.00 given under my hand and seal on the State this 28th day April 1920.

         W. Banks Dove
         Secretary of State
         (Seal)

Carhartt purchased about 2,000 acres of land on Red River Road and built Carhartt Mills Number 2 in 1916-1917. The mill was the most modern of its kind in the Carolinas. Nat Gaillard Walker, Rock Hill architect, designed the plans for the mill. There were three units with the first unit containing 3,600 spindles, 200 looms, and other complementary machinery. The three-story mill had a dye house, boiler rooms, and two warehouses. The outside was rubble stone or stucco with brick panels. The name Hamilton Carhartt was embedded in concrete above the main entrance to the mill. The name remained there until the mill was razed in 2001. It is said that the mill employed 2,000 to 3,000 employees. The number appears high as York County's population was only 50,000 in 1920.

Nat Gaillard Walker (1886-1946) was a well-known and highly respected American architect, born in South Carolina, and educated and trained in Charleston, South Carolina, and England. He designed buildings in Rock Hill, Charlotte, and Florida. He designed the London Business Building or London Printery Building at 125 Hampton Street, Rock Hill. The building was later known as White Printing Company. The building was owned by J. R. London, former Rock Hill mayor in the 1880s and president of two cotton mills in Rock Hill. Grace Lutheran Church on Oakland Avenue was designed by N. G. Walker and L. L. Hunter. In 1909, Walker designed the Carhartt Cotton Mills School Building. Walker had several buildings including a courthouse and a library listed on the National Register of Historic Places.

The Carhartt land is shown on the 1910 Jones and Walker map as Carhartt, South Carolina. The Southern railroad named the area Carhartt Station. The passenger station at Carhartt Station was less than desirable. More of a shed to protect from the rain, an effort was underway in 1920 with proper officials to provide an adequate station with telegraphic communications. The area later became known as Red River when Carhartt Mill No. 2 was sold to York Wilson. In 1946, Southern railroad renamed the area Celriver Station as Celanese bought the land formerly owned by Hamilton Carhartt, later L. W. Weil and Company, to build the Celriver Plant.

Following the Spanish Flu Epidemic of 1918 and World War I, the Global Recession of 1920-1921 greatly affected industrial activity in America and Europe. The Global Recession has often been called "The Forgotten Depression." Carhartt was forced to close both of his mills in Rock Hill in 1921. Carhartt owed $200,000 to John H. Cutter, a Charlotte cotton broker. In 1925, Carhartt signed over the Hamilton Carhartt Cotton Mills Number 1 to John Cutter as payment for his cotton debts. Carhartt Cotton Mills Number 2 was sold in 1925 to York Wilson. Charlie Cobb, President of People's National Bank in Rock Hill, chaired the committee to sell both mills in Rock Hill and Carhartt's cotton mill in Georgia. Carhartt placed his property in the hands of a creditor's committee and Charlie Cobb was chair of the committee, a group of men in whom Carhartt had confidence.

Partial Timeline
of Hamilton Carhartt Cotton Mills Number 2

Date	Register of Deeds
1916	Hamilton Carhartt Cotton Mills No. 2 Designed and Built in 1916-1917
1917	Book 44, page 266, January 12 Hamilton Carhartt Cotton Mills to Southern Railway Company, Right of Way
1921	Mill Closed because of 1920-1921 Global Recession
1925	Book 65, pages 41-44, October 15 Hamilton Carhartt Cotton Mills No. 2 Carhartt, SC Wylie W. Carhartt, President sold to Red River Cotton Mills York Wilson, W. M. Wilson, W. B. Wilson, A. C. Fennel, Daniel Heyward 100 Acres with Building and Equipment Recorded November 19, 1925 Book 65, page 19 Charter: Red River Cotton Mills

46

1925	Rock Hill, <u>The Evening Herald</u>, October 2, 1925 York Wilson plans to erect about 30 additional houses and to inaugurate both day and night shifts at the recently acquired Carhartt Mill No. 2.
1930	Idle in early 1930s
1944	Book 100, page 271, March 6, Deed to Real Estate William M. Wilson, Trustee to Hardin Mfg. Company #2 Red River Cotton Mills – York Wilson Mills Dan S. LaFar D. R. LaFar, Jr. (as Harden Mfg. Company) Harry Allen
1946	Southern Railway System renamed Carhartt Station to Celriver Station when Celanese bought the land formerly owned by Hamilton Carhartt.
2000	Closed in December
2001	Axel Demolition of Hillsborough, NC, demolished Carhartt Cotton Mills No. 2 in April after over 80 years of business. The name Hamilton Carhartt in concrete above the mill entrance remained until the mill was razed.

After Hamilton Carhartt Cotton Mills No. 2 was sold, it went through several owners and name changes including:

Red River Mill, Randolph Mill, Farmac Mill, Hardin Manufacturing.

Some Employees at Carhartt Mills No. 1 or Nor. 2
Rock Hill

Name	Occupation
Hamilton Carhartt Jr.	Vice-President and General Manager, Mill No.1 Hamilton Carhartt Sr. was President. In 1907, he turned the entire management of the mill over to his son
Wylie Welling Carhartt	President, Secretary, Treasurer
W. H. Harris, Philadelphia	General Manager
J. L. Adams	Resident Manager

B. L. Ivey	Assistant Treasurer
Lois Steele	Superintendent Carhartt School
Cammie Smith	Assistant to Miss Steele at Carhartt School
Amy Harrison	Secretary Community House, Mill No. 1
Amy Harrison	Kindergarten teacher, Mill No.1
Charlie Hailey	Boss man making 60 cents an hour
C. A. Drennan	Cotton grader and buyer
Howard Huddleston	
Lila Huddleston	
Etta Rayfield Walter Rayfield	
J. A. Adams	Superintendent
D. E. Mahaffey	Superintendent
C. W. Ross	Overseer of carding
W. S. Parker	Overseer of weave room
J. W. Davis	Second hand
W. F. Morton	Overseer of spinning
C. A. Moss	Machinist
R. R. Fry	Overseer cloth room
J. R. Huddleston	Overseer dye room
Mr. Green	Head bookkeeper and postmaster
W. M. Lybrand	Manager of company store
Cora Nicholson	Assistant manager company store, Mill No. 2
L. A. Pope	Built two houses to be used by workmen on the mill

Carrie Bell Poag	School principal, Mill No. 2
Nell Wood	Assistant teacher, Mill No. 2
E. L. Partridge	Resident manager in Atlanta, Georgia (formerly in Rock Hill)

1925 <u>Register of Deed:</u> Book 65, page 41, 100 Acres with Building and Equipment
Hamilton Carhartt Cotton Mills No. 2
sold to Red River Cotton Mills
State of South Carolina, County of York

KNOW ALL MEN BY THESE PRESENTS: THAT,
WHEREAS, Hamilton Carhartt Cotton Mills No. 2 is a corporation duly chartered under the laws of the State of South Carolina, with its principal place of business at Carhartt, in the County of York and State aforesaid.

AND,WHEREAS, at a meeting of the Board of Directors of Hamilton Carhartt Cotton Mills No. 2 held after due notice, on August 31st, 1925, a resolution was unanimously adopted by the Board of Directors setting forth that it was deemed for the best interest of the stockholders of Hamilton Carhartt Cotton Mills No. 2 that said corporation go into liquidation, wind up its affairs and dissolve, and to that end the Board of Directors recommended to the stockholders that all of the real estate, buildings, machinery, equipment, furniture and fixtures and all other property and assets of Hamilton Carhartt Cotton Mills No. 2, of every nature and description whatsoever, and also two certain strips of land adjoining the property of said Mill, upon one of which is located several houses built by said Mill and upon the other of which is located by the reservoir built by said Mill would be for the sum of One Hundred Thousand Dollars, to be due and payable fifteen thousand in cash which had been paid by the purchasers, eighteen thousand dollars on or before October 1st, 1925, and the balance with accrued interest there on from October 1st 1925 at the rate of six percent, per annum, payable annually until the whole be paid, due and payable one-half thereof, together with accrued interest on or before October 1st, 1916, and the remainder with accrued interest, as foresaid, on or before October 1st, 1927, provided, however, that the purchaser shall have the right to pay and settle the entire indebtedness representing the deferred payment above referred to at any time on or . . .

IN WITNESS WHEREOF, the said Hamilton Carhartt Cotton Mills No. 2 has caused these conveyances to be executed by Wylie W. Carhartt, its President and Benj. L. Ivey, its Secretary and Treasurer and its corporate seal to be hereto affixed this 15th day of October in the year of our Lord one thousand nine hundred and twenty-five and in the One Hundred and Fiftieth year of the Sovereignty and Independence of the United States of America.
Hamilton Carhartt Cotton Mills No. 2
By Wylie W. Carhartt, President

NOTE:
Hamilton Carhartt and his sons listed their homes as Carhartt, South Carolina, on land records and in the Rock Hill City Directories.

Rock Hill City Directories

Date	Info
1908-1909	Carhartt Hamilton pres. Hamilton Carhartt Cotton Mills New York City Cotton Mills Aragon Cotton Mills, north of city limits on main line Ry Arcade Mill, office 110-114 w Main Hamilton Carhartt Cotton Mills, 223 Chatham Ave Highland Park Manufacturing Co., e White nr city limits Lockmore Cotton Mills, Yorkville SC Manchester Cotton Mill (The), office 126 e Main Neely Mfg. Co., Yorkville SC Tavora Cotton Mills, Yorkville SC Victoria Cotton Mills, w Moore on So Ry Wymojo Yarn Mills, office 135 ½ e Main York Cotton Mills, Yorkville SC NOTE: The unusual name of Wymojo Mill was a combination of the last names of the owners: Wylie, Moore, Johnson.
1913-1914	Carhartt Hamilton, pres. Hamilton Carhartt Mfg, Detroit Mich Cotton Mills (Mfg. of Cotton Goods) Aragon Cotton Mills, n of city limits nr Sou RR Arcade Cotton Mills, end w Hagins Hamilton Carhartt Mills, 223 Chatham av cor White Harris Mills, Main nr Black Highland Park Mfg. Co, 869 Standard Manchester Cotton Mills, n of city limits on Sou RR Victoria Cotton Mills, w Moore on Sou RR Wymojo Yarn Mills w of city limits on Sou Ry

1917-1918	Carhartt Hamilton, pres. Hamilton Carhartt Cotton Mills, res **Carhartt S.C**.
	Carhartt Hamilton Jr., treas Hamilton Carhartt Cotton Mills, res Detroit Mich.
	Carhartt Hamilton Cotton Mills, exclusive high-grade denims, Chatham av cor w White, phone 268, Hamilton Carhartt pres, Hamilton Carhartt Jr, treas, Wylie Welling Carhartt sec Carhartt Wylie Welling, see Hamilton Carhartt Cotton Mills res Detroit, Mich
	Cotton Mills
	(Manufacturers of Cotton Goods)
	Aragon Cotton Mills n of city on Sou Ry
	Arcade Cotton Mills, end W Hagins
	Carhartt Hamilton Cotton Mills, Chatham Ave. cor w White
	Highland Park Mfg. Co 869 Standard
	Manchester Cotton Mills (Inc), n of city limits on Sou Ry
	Victoria Cotton Mills, w Moore on Sou Ry No 2, w Main extd
	Wymojo Yarn Mills, w of city limits on Sou Ry
1920-1921	Carhartt Hamilton, pres Hamilton Carhartt Cotton Mills, res Carhartt SC
	Carhartt Hamilton Jr. treas Hamilton Carhartt Cotton Mills, res Detroit Mich
	Carhartt Hamilton Cotton Mills, exclusive high-grade denims, Chatham av cor W White, phone 268, Hamilton Carhartt pres, Hamilton Carhart Jr v-pres, Wylie Welling Carhart sec-treas, B. L. Ivey asst treas Carhart Wylie Welling, sec-treas Hamilton Carhart Cotton Mills, res Detroit Mich
	Cotton Mills
	(Manufacturers of Cotton Goods)
	Aragon Cotton Mills n of city on Sou Ry
	Arcade Cotton Mills, end W Hagins
	Carhartt Cotton Mills, Chatham av cor w White
	Highland Park Mnfg Co 869 Standard
	Manchester Cotton Mills (Inc), n of city limits on Sou Ry
	Victoria Cotton Mill Railroad Ave. cor Moore
	Wymojo Yarn Mills, w of city limits on Sou Ry

1925-1926	Carhartt, Hamilton, pres Hamilton Carhartt Cotton Mills, res New York City
	Carhartt, Hamilton Cotton Mills denim mnfrs
	Chatham Ave cor White. Hamilton Carhartt pres,
	Hamilton Carhartt Jr. v- pres, Wylie Welling Carhartt sec-treas,
	B. L. Ivey asst treas
	Carhartt, Hamilton Jr. vice-pres,
	Hamilton Carhartt Cotton Mills
	Res Los Angeles Calif
	Carhartt Mills Community House, White cor Wilson,
	Miss Amy Harrison sec
	Carhartt Mills Kindergarten Wilson, Miss Amy Harrison tchr
	Carhartt Wylie W. Sec-tres, Hamilton Carhartt Cotton Mills
	res Detroit Mich
	Cotton Mills
	Arcade Cotton Mills, end W. Hagins
	Aragon-Baldwin (Aragon Plant), Cedar Rd.
	Hamilton Carhartt Cotton Mills Chatham cor White
	Helen Mills w White nr Stewart
	Highland Park Manufacturing Company 869 Standard
	Industrial Cotton Mills Co. (Inc.) cor Curtis and Swift
	Victoria Mills w Moore & Sou Ry w Main Extd
	Wymojo Mills, w White cor Stewart

The 1920-1921 Global Recession was brutal to manufacturers in both America and Europe. After World War I, returning troops created a surge in the labor force, unemployment peaked, and sells on manufactured goods went down dramatically. Manufactured goods in inventory dropped in value. The cost of living spiraled upward. Employers refused to recognize Unions and major work stoppages occurred. Manufacturing businesses in the United States and Europe went bankrupt. The fact that the Carhartt family kept their businesses alive in Atlanta, Detroit, and Dallas during the Global Recession and the Great Depression speaks to the strong character of the family and their concern for their employees. Carhartt survived until industry stabilized and he regained his worldwide presence.

**Hamilton Carhartt's work clothes labeled
"Made in Rock Hill, South Carolina,"
gave Rock Hill name recognition in the
United States, Canada, and Europe.**

CARHARTT PLANTATION

"I'm hungerin' to get away
Down yonder where the catfish play,
Down yonder where the skies are blue;
And every breeze that blows is true."
Hamilton Carhartt

The Plantation System in the South collapsed after the Civil War. Hamilton Carhartt with his descriptive and poetic writing style referred to the site of his family homes and farm on the Catawba River as the Carhartt Plantation. He created a three-mile stretch of unique homes with farmland for agriculture and animals. He was proud to call the site a plantation. He wrote a book entitled <u>Carhartt Plantation</u> where the "Sweet Catawba Flows and the Staple Cotton Grows." The booklet, yet to be located, is listed under several names: <u>Carhartt Plantation</u>, <u>The Old Plantation</u>, <u>The Plantation,</u> and the <u>Hamilton Carhartt Plantation</u>. Newspaper articles show that the mansion on the plantation was called several names including: Winter Home, Summer Home, Lodge, Inter Home, Bungalow; and Carhartt stated, "my own home." In many Carolina mill villages, houses were called bungalows. Bungalows were built for both small and large families. Rock Hillians called the houses in the mill villages, "mill houses."

Poetry written by Hamilton Carhartt and comments made by him that were reported in area newspapers cause one to believe that Carhartt found his "heart home" on the bank of the Catawba River. He found peace while listening to the river rush over the rocks and the songs of the birds in the trees, feeling the breeze cooled by the river and watching the silver starlight flicker on the traveling water. To walk over the Carhartt plantation site is to walk with the presence of peace.

Red River Road, off Cherry Road, had a county road leading to the Catawba River. At that end point, the Catawba River turned into a horseshoe curve offering a sweeping view of the river. Here on the bluff, Carhartt built his family homes and farm. This area has sandbanks and mudflats ideal for picnicking and play. Spratt Island was downriver with a foot bridge for crossing. Carhartt held picnics for his friends and employees on Spratt Island as well as at his home place.

The plantation site entrance from the county road had a barricade with a gate keeper building. A stone and tile archway led onto the cedar-tree lined drive. The embankment on each side of the drive was embedded with blue granite stone. On the right, one passed a flagpole, a stone silo, and other buildings. Carhartt was the first in Rock Hill to fly a flag over his mills. The American flag was flown at the plantation property entrance and a white flag was flown at the mansion entrance when Hamilton Carhartt was not receiving visitors. The gatekeeper knew when the white flag was flying to explain to the visitors that Mr. Carhartt was not receiving guests on that day.

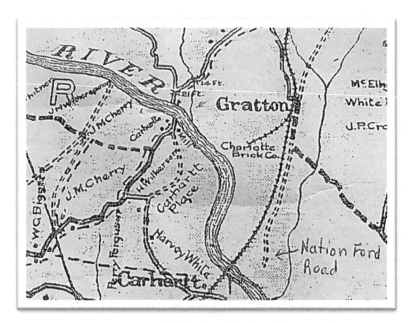

1910 Jones & Walker Map of York County
Carhartt Electrical/Grist Mill, Carhartt Plantation Site
Carhartt was between Rock Hill and Fort Mill.

Historical Center of York County, Culture and Heritage Museums
Map Available at McCelvey Center, 212 East Jefferson Street, York, South Carolina
Undated newspaper article located at McCelvey Center, York:
Mr. N. Gaillard Walker of Rock Hill was in Yorkville last Wednesday in company with Mr. J. J. Keller and had along with him several copies of the map of York County recently put in the market by his firm: Messrs. Jones and Walker. There has long been a sore and pressing need for a complete and satisfactory map that would show the township and school district lines, roads, rural free delivery routes, bridges, streams, schoolhouses and churches of York County, and this map seems to fill all these requirements and more because on it is to be found the location of almost every country home ...

The surveyors had the benefit of the original map of the county made in 1868 by Col. W. B. Allison, John G. Enroe, and Daniel Moore and of the soil survey map made by the federal government. It is in no sense, however, a copy of either of these works. Messrs. Jones and Walker went over the ground themselves, especially throughout the western part of the county and reviewed every line before they put it down. Their work is done with remarkable thoroughness. This map is simply invaluable to people who know how to appreciate such a work, but the published edition is limited, consisting of only three hundred. The expense of the survey and publication has been very heavy and under the circumstances the selling price of only $2.76 a copy is remarkably low. We think we do our readers a favor in advising all of them who want copies to write to Messrs. Jones and Walker at once ...

Cold-frame raised beds with stone spring house visible in back

Continuing on the driveway, one would pass the remains of a garage on the right that has old car parts in today's 2022. On the left one would see three cold-frame raised beds used by Joseph Bartha, horticulturist and estate manager, to propagate new plants. The remains of a stone one-room spring house are behind the beds, which provided water for the plants. The spring house had one level below ground with light wells. The light wells brought natural light into the lower level. Carhartt mentioned in a letter on 11 March 1918 to the Surgeon General in Washington, D.C., that water for the plantation was supplied by artesian wells and from natural mineral springs. He had the water analyzed and it was found to be above reproach. He had a concrete reservoir on the property and likely had drilled wells.

Hamilton Carhartt chose Winnsboro Blue Granite Stone to build his plantation homes and buildings along the Catawba River. Blue Granite Stone is South Carolina's State Stone and has been used for many buildings and monuments throughout the state including the 1908 South Carolina State House and Grace Lutheran Church on Oakland Avenue, Rock Hill. Blue Granite Stone was quarried from 1883-1946 in Winnsboro, South Carolina, and is known as Winnsboro Blue and Beautiful Blue. The stone is a light blue-gray color and used in construction and for decoration. Winnsboro was big in the granite mining industry using the Rockton and Rion Railway to ship the stone to other states. Winnsboro Blue Stone was donated to Shaw Air Force Base to be used for a monument to firefighters who served at New York City's "Ground Zero" on September 11, 2001.

Mansion
The Showplace and Social Scene of Rock Hill

A wrought-iron gate gave entrance to the driveway that encircled the mansion. The embankments were embedded in blue-gray stone. A path tiered from the front door of the mansion down the bluff to the river's edge. Steps were inlaid with flat-brown-river rocks.

Path from front porch down the bluff to the river's edge

Half-round front porch and columns holding the towering windows

The mansion, described as a fabulous showplace, had a half-circle front porch with a set of five steps on each side of the porch. The porch had six large columns. Porch and steps were covered with flat-brown-river rocks. The porch offered a nearly 360-degree view of the river with the river breeze spiraling up the bluff. Today, as you step over the threshold into the ruins, you enter a Door to the Past. You have entered a 44-foot-wide living room and facing a stone double-sided fireplace. The fireplace opened to the living room and to the room behind the living room. Mrs. Bartha Talbert, daughter of Joseph Bartha (horticulturist and estate manager), said in an article appearing in <u>The Evening Herald</u> on 12 August 1959 that the fireplace cost $10,000 when built. (Measurements on rooms and porches not exact.)

Covered and open-ended breezeway

A 10x54-foot covered and open-ended breezeway separated the ground-level living room from the lower-level bedrooms. Breezes singing through the trees and cooled by the river tunneled in and out of the breezeway. A set of 10 flat-rock steps descended from the living room to the bedrooms. The lower level was divided by a center hall from the breezeway to the side porch. Three bedrooms were in front of the hall with windows facing the river. The master bedroom had a double window and a single window. The adjacent two bedrooms had single windows. Two bedrooms and the 15x20-foot bathroom were on the back side of the hall. Each room appears to have had a fireplace according to the number of toppled stone chimneys.

Leo Nazareno Cullobosi, an Italian artist, was employed to come to Rock Hill, import green Italian tile, and inlay the tile in the impressive bathroom. The shower, with a beautiful etched glass door, had hot and cold running water. The bathtub, on the opposite side of the room, was surrounded by green tile. Mint green tile was used in the kitchens and baths of the houses on the plantation. Mr. and Mrs. Hamilton Carhartt were in Naples, Italy, in 1904. Perhaps they learned of Mr. Cullobosi on that trip.

1904 Packard Model L with Hamilton and Annette Carhartt in
Naples, Italy, in 1904. Hamilton Carhartt seated in front seat;
Annette Carhartt seated in back seat. Both are wearing light-colored coats.

The 14x36-foot side porch covered in flat-brown-river rocks had 10 columns with trees growing through the roof of the porch. A sundial in the area was arranged so that the North and the South hands did not separate. Carhartt did not want to express regional differences.

The living room had towering leaded-pane windows between the stately stone columns. The hardware on the window shutters was on the inside; therefore, the shutters would be flush with the exterior walls.

Light wells allow natural light to enter below ground areas.

The right wing of the house had a dining room over a 32x34-foot basement with four extending light wells. The basement had steps from the outside. The back area of the house is more difficult to define as the remains were pushed or have tumbled into piles of rubble covering the outline of rooms. A movie theater, always listed as for his family, friends, and employees, was at the back of the house. The movie theater converted to a ballroom for formal events. A room behind the living room that shared the dual fireplace had green tile, which meant a kitchen or a bath or both. A room above, creating a tri-level house, could have been used as living quarters for the cook. The cooking kitchen was detached from the house as was common during that period.

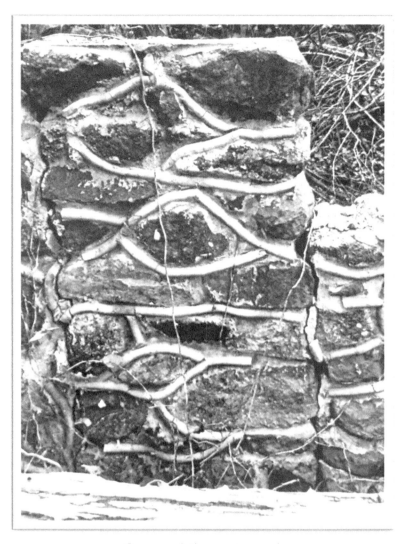

Convex pointing on stonework

The mansion, houses, and grounds were extremely labor-intensive. The pointing on the stone columns, foundations, and walls were hand-finished showing outstanding workmanship. The gathering of river stones for porches, steps, gardens, and bridle paths would have been greatly time-consuming.

Frank Owens (1865-1922) built the mansion. A Rock Hill carpenter and contractor, Frank Owens was held in high esteem and noted as one of the best-known residents of Rock Hill. He was a contractor in Rock Hill for years and many homes were built under his supervision. After his retirement, he continued to advise his friends who were planning to build. Frank and his wife Ida Catherine Gordon Owens (1866-1839) are listed in several Rock Hill City Directories as living on Elm Avenue, Marion

Street, and Carolina Street. Frank Owens later partnered with Franklin Sadler Love, and they became Love & Owens Contractors. Love & Owens Contractors built additions to Hamilton Carhartt Cotton Mills No. 1. Carhartt used local artisans and workers, giving an economic boost in those professions in Rock Hill.

The remains of a sizable house for his sons are near the mansion. At various times, both sons were active in the running of the two mills in Rock Hill and lived on the plantation site during those years as noted in the <u>Rock Hill City Directories</u>. There was a guest cottage called "The Briars." The guest house had a balcony built around a tree to avoid cutting the tree down. The balcony offered a bird's-eye view of the river and gardens. Hamilton Carhartt was a practicing environmentalist before it was cool to be an environmentalist.

Farmhouse on Carhartt Farm. Catawba River lower right.
1916 Postcard Courtesy of Mary Mallaney

Other known buildings on the plantation grounds:
As stated by Hamilton Carhartt in his letter to the Surgeon General on 18 March 1918, "the 1,400 acres has splendid outbuildings, farmhouses, tenant houses, gardener's cottage, dairy barn, mule barn, cattle barn, together with a herd of pure-blooded Guernsey cattle and seven saddle horses with full equipment for riding. All buildings are electric-lighted." Additionally, records show these buildings: the mansion, house for his sons and their families, guest house called The Briars, house for groundskeeper, green nursery with building, garage, silo, barn for Arabian horses, spring house, caretaker's house on farm, and concrete vats for wine production.

In 2019, Paul Gettys researched and wrote a paper on Joseph Bartha, horticulturist, who managed the estate and grounds of the Carhartt property. Paul wrote that Joseph Bartha, a native of Hungary, had a brother Peter who worked for Hamilton Carhartt as a gardener on Carhartt's massive estate. Peter secured a job with Mr. Carhartt for his brother Joseph who had training in landscape architecture and horticulture.

Peter Bartha did not speak English well but found a common language in German with Mr. Carhartt. Early 1900s' ship records show that Hamilton Carhartt made numerous trips to Europe. He likely learned foreign languages during his travels. In 1909, Carhartt traveled from New York to Liverpool, England, on the Lusitania (1907-1915). The Lusitania held the record for the fastest crossing of the Atlantic during that time and as the largest ship in the world. In 1915, a German U Boat torpedoed the Lusitania and 1,198 people drowned, which contributed to the United States entering WWI.

Joseph Bartha and his family came to America in 1907 and worked for Mr. Carhartt for 17 years beginning in 1909. After both Carhartt Mills closed, Joseph Bartha worked as a landscaper for Winthrop College on Oakland Avenue and St. Phillip's Hospital on North Confederate Avenue in Rock Hill. Joseph was noted as Rock Hill's horticultural authority.

Bartha designed the total acreage of the Carhartt Plantation. His work included laying out walks at the mansion, using river stones for the borders. He planted a number of varieties of trees and shrubs and had elaborate English gardens. When Mr. Carhartt built part of the house, Joseph arranged for the porches to be built around trees. There was a green nursery on site, where Bartha propagated plants, trees, and shrubs, when possible, using native species: Paul Scarlet roses, Barbary hedges, catalpa trees, and a variety of cedars. He operated a regular nursery, utilizing whenever possible native growth and plants. Hamilton Carhartt's vision of a home on the bank of the Catawba River became a reality through the talent and skill of Joseph Bartha. The area became a place of beauty, order, and quiet contentment.

Rock Hill, The Evening Herald, July 1, 1914
At Carhartt Bungalow
A most enjoyable outing of Tuesday was the picnic at the river given jointly by a number of young people of the city. Two large wagons carried the party out at an early hour and the day was spent in the enjoyment of all the delights of such an occasion, not the least of which was the appetizing dinner spread 'neath the trees' of the "island." Mr. and Mrs. A. E. Hutchison were the chaperones, the others composing the party being Misses Kathryn Beach, Annie Reid Poag, Marie Steele, Dorothy Tompkins, Ruth Youngblood, Leona Moore, Nan Roddey, Margaret McElwee, Kathryn McElwee, Louise Flowers, Isabel Boyd, Helen Fewell, Nannie Lee Sowell, Sue Ramsey Johnston, Elizabeth Pressley, Christine Cowan, Ed Base, Sam Barber, Tally Albert, Bernard Young, Hazel Youngblood, Ed Brown, Sam Brice, J. J. Waters, Perry Gill, William Shurley, Fletcher Kuykendall, Clarence Kuykendall, Lindsey Mill, and Haskell Turner.

Remains at Garage Site on Plantation

Flat River-Rock cover porches and steps

Farm

Hamilton Carhartt, a man of wide-ranging activities, was one who would settle for nothing less than the best. When he bought multi-acres along the west and east sides of the Catawba River, he created a showcase farm. He owned three miles on the west side of the Catawba River from the present-day Highway 21 bridge to the now-Norfolk Southern Railroad Trestle and beyond.

65

Farm building on Carhartt Farm
1916 Postcard Courtesy of Mary Mallaney

The Farm, though a showplace, was also a working agricultural farm with alfalfa, corn, cotton, a dairy farm, grape vineyard, and raising pheasants for stocking game preserves. Mr. Carhartt enjoyed bird hunting. He and his neighbor, William Campbell Hutchison, hunted birds on horseback on their adjoining lands; a story still told in the Hutchison family. Carhartt fenced his pastures with concrete posts, unusual in the Carolinas. During these years, Rock Hill was known as "the Alfalfa Center of the Southeast." The area was dependent on cotton, but cotton removes large quantities of nutrients from the soil. Alfalfa is a highly nutritious feed for cattle and replenishes nutrients in the cotton-poor soil.

Common and not-so-common animals were on the Farm: Polo and Shetland ponies, Berkshire hogs, Shropshire sheep, Guernsey milk cattle, Hereford beef cattle, White Wyandotte and Rhode Island Red poultry, Japanese Silkies for pheasant egg hatching, Carneaux pigeons, Belgian hares, Angora goats, imported white and domestic peafowls, and the internationally recognized Arabian horses.

> "Out at Carhartt's, where the Corneaux pigeons fly
> And the tiny Shetland ponies romp and play."
> Hamilton Carhartt

There were several large, circular, concrete grape vats where grapes were stomped by foot. If you desire to make wine and lack a wine press, try crushing grapes using this ancient method. Bacteria will not survive in the wine because of the alcohol content.

Hamilton Carhartt owned the land facing Cherry Road and leased that land to the group who formed the first golf club in Rock Hill, the Catawba River Golf Club. The club was located on the right on Highway 21 North near the Catawba bridge. Porter's Grill was later built on the opposite side of the highway.

Rock Hill, The Herald, August 31, 1925
The Catawba River Golf Club was organized about eight years ago and received a lease from Hamilton Carhartt for property near the Catawba Bridge. The lease will expire in a year or two.

Rock Hill, The Herald, May 20, 1931
The Catawba River Golf Club had a tournament yesterday. R. H. Jones of Rock Hill took first place, J. L. Spratt of Fort Mill took second place, and Ed Allen of Rock Hill took third place. The group had a picnic supper in the grove adjoining the club house. W. B. Avery, the Manager and Treasurer, reported the finances were in good condition. The matter of buying a permanent site for the club was discussed.

Wilmington, North Carolina, The Wilmington Morning Star, April 28, 1915
The country around Rock Hill is filling up with improved cattle and hogs and steps are being taken to introduce the business of raising horses and mules on the farms. Among those who are particularly interested in good horses is Hamilton Carhartt, the well-known manufacturer of this city and Detroit, Michigan, who is introducing Arabian stock in this section. Mr. Carhartt has at his farm on the Catawba river, a few miles from Rock Hill, a fine Arabian stallion, desert bred, an animal that is attracting much attention and admiration. On behalf of the great number of citizens of this county and section of the State who are laboring for the diversification of agriculture, for the introduction of stock raising and the improvement of farm animals, The Herald desires to commend the efforts of Mr. Carhartt. He is a citizen of a distant State but because of local manufacturing and farming interest, feels it his duty to unite with the citizens of this section in promoting the great movement for agricultural development which is daily gaining force and showing results throughout this part of the State. Rock Hill, South Carolina, Herald.

Fort Mill Times, August 1, 1918
A hailstorm visited the farm of Hamilton Carhartt, on the Catawba, Sunday afternoon between five and six o'clock, damaging about fifty acres of cotton and corn. The extent of the damage is not yet known, but Mr. Poag states in some cases the damage will be considerable. The hailstorm appeared to dip down and strike the Carhartt plantation, passing on up the river. It is not known whether other farmers suffered losses.

Pure-blooded Guernsey cows grazed the pastures at Carhartt Dairy Farm. Guernsey cows are known for producing high-protein and flavorful milk on pasture alone with no grain. They are big milk producers. York County had several dairy farms in the early 1900s but federal and state regulations requiring raw milk to be pasteurized forced some area dairies out of business. Pasteurization is a process using heat to kill bacteria in raw milk.

Carhartt Farm Management:
R. S. Poag, Superintendent of Farm
Marvin Poag, Superintendent, hired November 1907
John Hayes, Farm
S. H. Blake, Carpentry and Mechanical Supervisor

Rock Hill, The Herald, June 21, 1941
A large barn on the Weil Farm, the old Carhartt Place on the Catawba River, was destroyed by fire last night, Manager Bob Oates said today. They lost 400 bushels of oats, 75 bushels of wheat and five tons of hay.

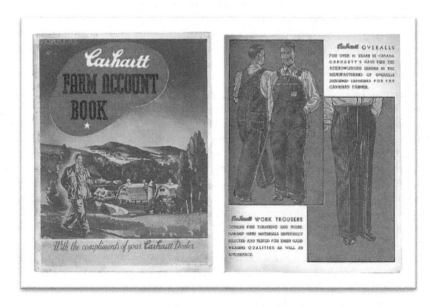

Arabian Stallion Breeding Program

Arabian Stallion Houran

Betty Hill Rankin, on a walk to talk about the historic places along the Riverwalk Trail, gave me printed information on the Arabian horses that Carhartt bred on his farm including a picture of Carhartt's internationally known foundation Arabian stallion, Houran.

Betty says that Houran was a "big deal" in the Arabian horse world as he was desert-bred in 1904 by A Kuhaylan 'Ajuz and was one of the stallions imported from Turkey by Homer Davenport in 1906. After Davenport died in 1912, Houran was owned by Davenport's financial partner, Peter Bradley of Hingham Stock Farm, until after the 1914 breeding season. Carhartt mentioned his Arabian stallion, Houran, in a January 6, 1916, <u>Fort Mill Times</u> article. Carhartt said his specialty was breeding Arabian horses. Houran is number 26 in the <u>Arabian Horse Registry</u>. Records show that Houran was on the Carhartt Farm in 1915. Houran was started at stud six years after importation.

The following information provides insight into the importance of Hamilton Carhartt's little-known legacy of owning one of the Davenport stallions and establishing a breeding program in Rock Hill, South Carolina.

Arabian horses in America were basically unknown until the 1893 World's Fair in Chicago when the Ottoman Empire sent a delegation with Arabian horses. This display triggered a desire on the part of Homer Davenport to go to Turkey to acquire desert-bred Arabians. The export of Arabian horses, especially mares, was rare and required special permission from the Ottoman Sultan, Abdul Hamid II. With help from President Theodore Roosevelt, that permission was granted in 1906. Davenport, with financial assistance from Peter Bradley, went to Turkey to import 27 Arabian horses including the two-year-old stallion, Houran. This led to the organization of The Arabian Horse Club of America. Hamilton Carhartt was a member of the association and had horses registered in the Arabian Stud from 1918 to 1922.

Resources:
https://www.wiwfarm.com/The_Davenport_Arabian_How_they_came_to_be.ht m

Lists the 27 Davenport Arabians (17 stallions and 10 mares). Mares were valued more at the time because the lineage was traced through them.

Chief Feature of the Carhartt Plantation: Houran, Arabian Stallion
Foaled: January 1904 AHR 26

Davenport Foundation Stallion Houran was the sire of Bint Nimnaarah. He was bred to a Davenport mare named Nimnaarah. The foal was born in 1918.

Daughters of the Wind: a blog on desert Arabian Horses, past and present.
    Houran, Kuhaylan Tamri by Edouard Aldahdad
    Posted on March 12th, 2010
    Houran left only one daughter in asil USA breeding (the Ma'naghiyah Sbayliyah mare Bint Nimnaarah). Houran was sired by a Hadban Enzahi stallion of the Anazah tribes, some branches of which were home to many Hadban Enzahi marabit, such as Hadban Mushaytib, the most respected.

NOTE:
Bint means "daughter of" in Arabian horse names. Carhartt's Bint Nimnaarah 452 was the daughter of Davenport foundation mare Nimnaarah.

Color B = Bay; CH = Chestnut. The Arabian lines are through the mares.

Table 1: The First Four Generations of Descent from Leopard 233,
by Michael Bowling
Published in the <u>Arabian Horse World</u>, July 1979
The Descent of Anazeh Table I:

Name	AHR Number	Color	Sex	Year Foaled	Breeder
BINT NIMNA ARAH	452	B	F	1918	Hamilton Carhartt Rock Hill, SC
SIMRI	453	B	F	1920	Hamilton Carhartt
HAARA NMIN	451	B	F	1921	Hamilton Carhartt
NIMHO URA	543	B	F	1922	Hamilton Carhartt

NIMNAARAH, fortunately for the sanity of pedigree readers, passed into the hands of Hamilton Carhartt of South Carolina, who bred four outcross foals (at least that many; note that only fillies are registered, suggesting the possibility of colts that may have dropped out of sight) from her by the desert-bred HOURAN, a Kehilan Tamri imported by Davenport. The next step is uncertain, but it appears that two NIMNAARAH daughters, HAARANMIN 451 and BINT NIMNAARAH 452, went to Traveler's Rest with General J. M. Dickinson for a brief stay, during which BINT NIMNAARAH was bred to Dickinson's ANTEZ. At any rate in 1932 both foaled fillies for John A. George of Indiana–BINT NIMNAARAH produced the ANTEZ daughter YDRISSA 947, and HARAANMIN produced the RIBAL daughter OURIDA 946, RIBAL being the John A. George herd sire at that time. https://archive.gyford.com/2009/04/28/www.geocities.com/Heartland/Estates/ 3095/TheForgottenMan.html

The Forgotten Man, Peter Bradley's Role in Early American Breeding
by Charles and Jeanne Craver, <u>American Horse World</u>, July 1984.

"Carhartt's Life Was More Than Textiles."
Betty Hill Rankin

NOTE:
Hamilton Carhartt gifted an Arabian stallion, Heranmin, to Dr. William Wallace Fennell of Fennell Infirmary of Rock Hill as a love gift for medical services. Dr. Fennell was a noted surgeon of outstanding ability. Mr. Carhartt credits Dr. Fennell for providing medical attention to him at a serious time of need. (Unable to locate exact situation.)

Russ Frase, Historic Preservationist who has restored Dr. W. W. Fennell's home, told me that Hamilton Carhartt gave a Shetland Pony, named Stoney (or Sonny) to Dr. Fennell's son, Buck Fennell.

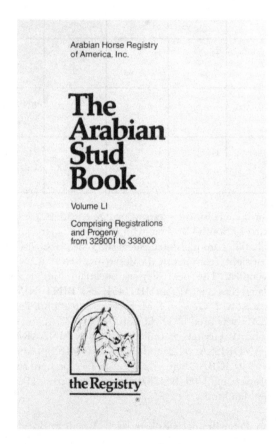

Arabian Horse Registry
of America, Inc.

**The
Arabian
Stud
Book**

Volume LI

Comprising Registrations
and Progeny
from 328001 to 338000

the Registry

Carhartt had horses registered in <u>The Arabian Stud Book</u> from 1918-1922

Jones Grist Mill and
Carhartt Electrical and Grist Mill
(Carhartt converted the mill in 1908 to produce electrical power for his plantation.)

Books and articles state the presence of Garrison Mill at the location where Edgar Jones in 1902 built a mill on the foundation of the said Garrison Mill. I have not located a deed or documentation of any sort for Garrison Mill on the west side of the Catawba River. The Isaac Garrison and Theodoric Webb Grist Mill is well documented on Steele Creek in Fort Mill on the east side of the Catawba River. Garrison could have leased land on the west side of the Catawba River or maybe he was the miller, and the Grist Mill came to be known by his name or other reasons that records are not easily available. Records show that the grist mill was known as Harris-McCullough Mill in 1874. The Jones Family bought the mill from James W. Harris in 1873.

William Bradford Jr. writes in his book <u>Out of the Past</u> that the "Fort" in Fort Mill is named for a colonial-era fort started but never finished by the British to protect the Catawba Indians from their enemies, the Shawnees, the Delaware, and the Iroquois Indians. The Historical Marker is on Brickyard Road near Spratt Cemetery. The "Mill" in Fort Mill is named for Webb's Grist Mill on Steele Creek.

Webb's Grist Mill. Photo from <u>Out of The Past</u> by William R. Bradford, Jr.
Drawing by Ken Whitsett, used as masthead of <u>The Fort Mill Times</u> in mid-1950s

73

Man-made sluice directing water to the waterwheel

The Edgar Jones Grist Mill was in operation from 1902 to 1908. The mill site also provided ferry services. Hamilton Carhartt bought the Jones Grist Mill in 1908 and converted it to produce electricity for his plantation on the bluff above the mill.

The mill was located below the now-Highway 21 bridge. The man-made sluice that directed water to the waterwheel on the river embankment is visible on the Riverwalk Trail with the head race directing water into the mill ruins and the tail race returning the water to its normal course. A beautiful early engineering sight. Foundational remains of the mill are visible on the bank of the river and on the incline where the grist mill once stood.

During the 1916 Great Flood, the mill and waterwheel were lifted from their foundations and swept intact about a mile down river until they became lodged in a bend of the river and eventually broke and were carried down the river. Catawba Power Company provided a plentiful source of electricity as soon as clean-up was completed after the flood.

The source of the Catawba River is in Old Fort, North Carolina, and it drops over 6,000 feet before it empties into the Atlantic. The drop in elevation was perfect for the grist mill industry along the 450 miles of the Catawba River's run to the sea. Grist mills were the leading industry in the South before textile mills. The Catawba River had a name change to Wateree River as it entered Big Wateree Creek. The river now has eleven dams plus several reservoirs. The river is a link-of-lakes rather than a river.

Headwaters of Catawba River, Old Fort, North Carolina

The first dam on the Catawba River built a couple of miles up-river from the Carhartt Plantation became operative in 1904 with the goal to provide electricity to the mills in Rock Hill as quickly as possible. Victoria Mill (formerly Globe Mill) was the first mill to have electrical power from the Catawba Hydro Station of the Catawba Power Company (now Duke Energy). Electricity had not yet been distributed to the area of the Carhartt Plantation.

Before the 1904 dam was built, the river was filled with migratory fish that traveled between the sea and the river. Fish that lived in fresh water and spawned in salt water and fish that lived in salt water but spawned in fresh water. In Colonial times, the inland river was a migratory path for tens of thousands of sturgeons, shad, and herring. Records exist for these fish being in Bullock's and Stephen's Creeks, Broad River, and the Catawba River as far up as Marion, N.C.

The Catawba Indians built fish weirs or fish dams. The fish weirs were made of large rocks placed in the shape of a W or a V. The Catawba Indian Fish Weir upstream from the Nation Ford Railroad Trestle is made in a double V-shaped trap. The fish weir was placed on the National Record of Properties in March 2007. The fish were funneled into gaps between the rocks making it easier for the Indians to catch great quantities in baskets or nets. For the sturgeon, the Catawba Indians used harpoons made of fire-hardened bamboo cane. Commercial fishing along the Catawba used nets strung across the river. The fish would be cleaned, processed, salted, and packed in wooden barrels for shipment. The 1825 Atlas of SC created by Robert Mills shows fisheries on the Catawba River: Lacky's Fishery and Wall's Fishery. Both were located north of the Great Falls of the Catawba River near Fishing Creek.

The decline in fish population had to do with the settlers clearing land and growing crops. Erosion of topsoil and mud into the river had a detrimental impact on fish habitat. Then in 1784, construction of diversion dams for grist mills reduced the seasonal migration of shad, herring, sturgeon, eel, and striped bass. The Fort Mill Times reported in May 1908 that a six-foot-long, 117-pound sturgeon was caught at Carhartt Mill. The sturgeon had been trapped between the 1904 dam and Fishing Creek and could not escape.

In 1908, Carhartt bought the Jones active grist mill, which was adjacent to his river property. He converted the mill to produce electricity for his plantation houses and continued the operation of the grist mill and the ferry. Electricity was later distributed to his Mill No. 2, Plantation and English Village from the Catawba Power Company.

The only free-flowing section of the Catawba River flows by the old plantation site. It is still a place where you leave your stress behind. This 30-mile free-flowing portion extending from the Lake Wylie Dam to SC Highway 9 Bridge was designated as a State Scenic River in 2008 and gained a 50-foot Riparian Zone thanks to an effort initiated by the Henry's Knob Group of Sierra Club in the early 1990s that resulted in the Catawba River Corridor Plan published in 1994. Though free flowing, the water level is controlled by Duke Energy. The Catawba River flows red from the run-off of the iron oxide in York County's red clay.

The Jones-Carhartt Mill was on 129 acres of property that has a story of its own as it transfers from one Jones family member to another. The earliest records located are 1873 with the 129 acres remaining among the Jones Family until sold to Carhartt in 1908. The tract became a part of Hamilton Carhartt's plantation and later transferred through several owners and now is known as Riverwalk.

Riverwalk, a riverfront community on Riverwalk Parkway off Cherry Road
(Former Carhartt Plantation)

Records of the Jones and Carhartt Mill
York County Government Center
6 South Congress Street, York, South Carolina
<u>Register of Deeds</u>

1873	Book Y, page 507, 129 Acres along Catawba River James W. Harris sold to Isaac Jones
1874	Book Z, page 315, 129 Acres on west side of Catawba River sold to J. C. Jones Known as Harris-McCullough Mill Recorded: January 11, 1875
1885	Book C 5, page 409, January 28, 128 Acres +- J. C. Jones sold to W. I. Jones Recorded: January 28, 1885
1906	Book 26, page 573, November 15 A. O. Jones et al. sold to W. H. Jones, Heirs of W. J. Jones

1906   Book 26, page 575, 129 Acres on Catawba River,
November 15
W. H. Jones et al.
sold to Edgar Jones
Edgar Jones one of heirs in the settlement of the estate of
W. J. Jones, deceased. Edgar Jones had two-thirds interest
in the property.

1908   Book 43, page 315, 129 Acres on Catawba River
W. J. Jones recorded October 8, 1885
sold to Edgar Jones from other family members

1908   Book 36, page 563, 129 Acres on Catawba River
Edgar Jones sold to Hamilton Carhartt tract of land,
waterpower, ferry, mill. Adjoining land of A. E.
Hutchison. Bounded by Wilkerson, Carhartt, Catawba
River and others. Land bought in 1908 for $7,500.
Recorded June 24, 1912.

1925   Plat Book 2, page 574 (two pages)
T. E. McMakin, Clerk of Court York County
sold to Lawrence W. Weil and John H. Weil
Public Auction, that certain plantation or tract of land . . .
1,089 Acres Recorded: February 11, 1925

1945   Book 119, page 137, 129 Acres on Catawba River
J. Harry Weil et al., Weil Cotton Company et al.
sold to Ethel K. Moore Being same land conveyed by
Edgar Jones to Hamilton Carhartt in Deed Book 36,
page 563 The Edgar Jones tract of Carhartt property.
Surveyed 1908 by W. W. Miller August 16, 1945.
Recorded: September 8, 1945

1946   Book 123, page 87, 129 Acres on Catawba River,
February 2, Ethel K. Moore sold to Celanese Corporation
for $5,805 Bounded by Bynum, Wilkerson and Weil lands
Land formerly belonged to James Melton Cherry
Being the same land conveyed by Edgar Jones
to Hamilton Carhartt on June 24, 1912
Recorded in Book 36, page 565.
Surveyed in 1908 by W. W. Miller. Edgar Jones sold to
Hamilton Carhartt in 1908, Recorded 1912.

Rock Hill, The Evening Herald, May 25, 1901
On the 20-21st, a rainstorm hit the area lasting 38 hours. The railroad bridge and
Garrison's Mill were visited by hundreds of persons to see the damage. Garrison's
Mill was moved slightly from its foundation.

Fort Mill Times, January 29, 1902

The Times has been reliably informed that within a few weeks a roller mill, equipped with the latest improved machinery, will be opened at the Jones mill site on Catawba River near Spratt's Island. The promoters of the enterprise are Messrs. W. I. and Edgar Jones and the Misses Harris, of Fort Mill township. An up-to-date roller mill is a thing which Fort Mill Township has needed for a number of years and now that one is to be built by Fort Mill people, the farmers of the township should show an appreciative spirit by giving it their undivided support.

Rock Hill, The Herald, April 2, 1902
The Jones' Roller Mill

Mr. Edgar Jones was in town last Saturday and stated to The Herald that definite steps are being taken to erect the roller mill at the old Garrison mill site. The old building, which was erected in 1845, has been torn down, and lumber has been hauled to the river for the new structure. It will be 24 by 32 feet, two stories in height and will be built on the foundations of the old building. The machinery in the flouring department will be new and of the latest models, the roller mill having a capacity of about 30 barrels of flour per day. The burr in the old mill will be used for meal in the new. Mr. Edgar Jones will be associated with his uncle Mr. W. I. Jones, and they have decided to establish a ferry at the mill. The flat to be used there is now being made. Mr. Jones says that will be the nearest possible way from Rock Hill to Fort Mill and anticipates a great deal of travel over his ferry.

Rock Hill, The Herald, December 13, 1902
New Advertisements
The Jones Roller Mill on the river will grind your corn Tuesdays and Fridays.

Rock Hill, The Herald, May 20, 1903
An outing was held at Garrisons' Mill on the banks of the Catawba River. The group from Rock Hill included: Mr. and Mrs. J. B. Heath, Mr. and Mrs. S. T. Frew, Dr. and Mrs. W. W. Fennell, Mrs. R. P. Boyd, and the Misses Pauline Mullins and Johnson.

Fort Mill Times, 30 January 1908
Carhartt bought the Jones roller mill property on the river for about $10,000. He plans to install electric generators in the mill of sufficient power to light that building and his handsome summer home on the Whitner place about a half mile down the river.

Fort Mill Times, August 18, 1910
The Times was incorrect in our report that the Carhartt Roller Mill, formerly Jones' Mill, on the Catawba River two miles from Fort Mill had closed and that the use of the Ferry had been discontinued as a result of the death of the miller and ferryman. The mill is running daily and is prepared to grind the community's wheat and corn as usual.

Ruins of Grist Mill on embankment of Catawba River

Within the most recent year, soil washed away from backside of Grist Mill

The 1916 Great Flood

Two hurricanes, one from Alabama and one from the Pee Dee basin, collided and stalled in the Carolinas in July 1916 with high winds and record rainfalls. Water levels on the Catawba River reached record highs. Flooding and great damage extended through the Carolinas to the coast. Every highway bridge and all nine railway trestles on the Catawba were swept away. Flood waters demolished barns, houses, uprooted trees, swept away bales of cotton, goods stored in warehouses, livestock, fowl, snakes, and watermelons. River bottom crops were destroyed, and rich topsoil washed away. Water-powered grist mills and cotton mills up and down the river were destroyed along with grain and cotton crops. Timbers, parts of houses, bales of cotton, crops, and good soil were carried down the river. The early death count mounted as communications opened to other parts of the Carolinas. Rock Hill was almost completely isolated from the rest of the country.

Farmhouse on Carhartt Farm. 1916 Great Flood
Postcard Courtesy of Mary Mallaney

Rock Hill, <u>The Evening Herald</u>, July 1916, Coverage of The Great Flood

SATURDAY, JULY 15, 1916

The story of the storm would not be complete without mentioning the fact that the city street sweeper was on the job as usual this morning, regardless of the fact that the wind and rain had thoroughly cleaned the asphalt pavements. Now, it is generally known that the city some time ago attached a sprinkling arrangement to the sweeper to lay the dust while sweeping. The driver, with an umbrella and a slicker to turn the constant downpour, was driving along unconcernedly his sprinkling attachment in full operation as if the street was really dusty. Or was it imagination that the pavement was really wet.

The Rock Hill mills are practically out of commission and there is little likelihood of their being started during this week. The Arcade and the Manchester have steam plants and are being partially operated. The Aragon, Wymojo, and Victoria are idle, not having any steam plant. The Highland Park has a steam plant and only partial operation is possible. The Carhartt Mill is idle, having no steam plant. The loss to each of the local mills will amount to thousands of dollars provided they are closed down this week only. If the time is extended the loss will be greater, of course. And the same will be true of all other mills dependent upon the power company for power.

SUNDAY, JULY 16, 1916

Worst flood in history of Carolinas.
Fort Mill Road bridge gave way on Sunday.

MONDAY, JULY 17, 1916

Roddey Bridge washed away. (John T. Roddey bridge, built 1912)
Travel stopped. Telegraph, mail, telephone and train travel stopped.
Hundreds of bales of cotton came floating down the river.
Southern Power Company out of business plus anything depending on electricity.

Southern Loses Three Bridges:
The bridge of the Southern over the main line between Rock Hill and Charlotte gave way beneath the terrific strain this morning at 5:30 o'clock, several sections giving way. The last of the bridge tumbled at 9:30 o'clock.

Photo Courtesy of Crystal Grant Mead

The railroad trestle at Nation Ford was the largest of the trestles to wash away. The Nation Ford trestle stands 50 feet above water with a length of 1,127 feet. Three trestles have been built on the original pylons built by Frederick and Horace Nims.

19 April 1865: Trestle burned by the Stoneman's Raid Campaign. General George Stoneman's orders were "to destroy but not to fight." General William Jackson Palmer was charged with the responsibility to destroy the railroads. He ordered Major Erastus Cratty Moderwell to burn the Nation Ford trestle. The trestle was burned from the Fort Mill side and two cannons on the Rock Hill side were made inoperable and pushed into the Catawba River. In 1999, the Nation Ford Land Trust preserved the 0.3-acre Confederate Gun Pit site on the Rock Hill side of the river. Stoneman's Raid destroyed more than 30 bridges in the Carolinas and the Catawba River trestle was the largest.

TUESDAY, JULY 18, 1916
Carhartt Mill Gave Way Monday Afternoon
Monday afternoon at 5 o'clock, the Carhartt mill left its foundation and floated down the river. It progressed about a mile, lodging in the bend of the river. It was almost entirely submerged when the water floated it from the foundation. The mill has been standing more than half a century, as evidence that the water is much higher than ever before.

83

Carhartt Electrical and Grist Mill. River running behind buildings.
1916 Great Flood
Postcard Courtesy of Mary Mallaney

WEDNESDAY, JULY 19, 1916

Southern Railway is working on gathering materials to repair the trestle at Nation Ford. The wrecking crew is out removing remains of the trestle. River will rise for weeks yet.

Transfer Passengers Across the River

Secretary Timmons stated this afternoon that arrangements had been made by U.M. Pursley to transfer passengers across the river, at a point above the railroad bridge. Mr. Henderson gave permission to go through private grounds of **Hamilton Carhartt**, in order that a suitable landing place might be secured. It was said Mr. Pursley would have several bateaus in service this afternoon. (A bateau is a shallow, flat-bottomed boat.)

THURSDAY, JULY 20, 1916

RUSHING WORK ON BRIDGES OVER THE CATAWBA

The work of putting up a temporary bridge across the Catawba is progressing as rapidly as possible. The Southern has an immense force on the job, but it will be some days before the trestle will be in shape for service. A new steel bridge has already been ordered for the river. The Catawba at this point is more than a thousand feet wide, steel framework having been torn down for that distance.

FERRY ACROSS CATAWBA IS BADLY NEEDED
and Chamber Committee is Hard at Work on the Proposition.
The transportation committee of the Chamber of Commerce A. H. Bynum, chairman; W. M. Dunlap, T. O. Flowers, J. K. Roach, Jas. N. Benton and Secretary Timmons is quite active in an effort to provide means of crossing the Catawba river between here and Fort Mill, pending the erection of the county bridge. A meeting was held yesterday afternoon and the committee visited the river with a view of ascertaining whether it would be practical to establish a ferry near the railroad bridge. The many rocks in the river at this point make it impractical to attempt such and the mud on each side of the river would necessitate the construction of a roadway for several hundred yards on either side of the river.

This morning a committee went out to the location of the county bridge to consider the advisability of establishing a ferry at this point. R. A. Stone and U. M. Pursley accompanied the committee to this point. If it is decided that such a venture would be feasible Mr. Pursley will immediately begin to operate a ferry, providing means for vehicles and automobiles to operate between Rock Hill and Fort Mill, thus giving immediate communication with the north. Formerly there was a ferry near the site of the old **Carhartt Mill**, but it would be necessary to build a number of bridges on the other side, hence this is impractical at the present time.

SOUTHERN WILL TRANSFER MAILS
AND PASSENGERS ACROSS CATAWBA
Two Trains Daily Will Exchange Passengers at **Carhartt Station**.
The Southern Railway officially announced today that beginning tomorrow morning passengers will be transferred by boat at the Catawba River for two trains operating on the regular schedule. These are train No. 36, northbound at 8:35 a.m. and train No. 31 southbound at 7:35 a.m. No baggage will be handled across the river and no express will be transferred. The mails will be handled on these trains and transferred across the river, but this does not include parcel post mail. A transfer will be made at the river this afternoon, for today only, and passengers will come over this line for the first time since the bridge was destroyed. Workmen were busy today creating walkways to the river for the passengers.

While the trestles and bridges were being rebuilt, Catawba Indians led by John Brown and Jim Sanders, a Carlisle College graduate, operated small row boats, establishing a ferry service to carry mail, passengers, and goods back and forth in the tri-county area of York, Chester, and Lancaster.

Rebuilding of railroad train trestle
Photo Courtesy of Crystal Grant Mead

The old Nation Ford Crossing directly beneath trestle.
Norfolk Southern rail line active today.
Trestle was on Carhartt Plantation site and named Carhartt Station until 1946.

MONDAY, JULY 24, 1916
Workmen are busy repairing damage wrought by floods
Railroad Trestles going up and Southern Power lines being rebuilt; still too early to learn damage to crops, rains are continuing . . .

Would Put Bridge at End of the Cherry Road
Already a movement is on foot to have a bridge span the Catawba at the end of the Cherry Road, thus cutting off several miles of the distance between here and Fort Mill. Now that a new bridge will have to be built, it is being urged that it be placed where it will be of the greatest convenience and those favoring the new location believe this will be favored by the large majority of those affected. Not only will it materially shorten the distance between here and Fort Mill, but it will provide a much better highway.

In addition to the plan to build a new bridge at a more convenient location, the destruction of bridges created a great boom in the lumber business.

Broad River, the western border of York County, was also running wild.

Carhartt Plantation Sold, Resold and Resold

The Global Recession of 1920-1921 greatly affected the manufacture of goods in both America and Europe. Hamilton Carhartt was forced to close and sell both of his mills in Rock Hill, the Carhartt plantation, both mill villages, and other properties yet to be developed. The sales were in 1924 and 1925. His holdings in Rock Hill, once great, were gone with the Global Recession.

The causes of the Global Recession and the effect on manufacturers is written at the end of the Carhartt Mills chapter.

Rock Hill, South Carolina, Historical Research Committee Papers, #14
Submitted by Mr. C. L. Cobb Sr.
The Celanese Corporation of America purchased the Carhartt Plantation which formed the greater part of land acquired by them for their Celriver site. At one time the Southern Railroad Station was known as Carhartt, South Carolina, but was later changed to Red River when Carhartt Mill No. 2 became known as Red River Cotton Mill owned by York Wilson and C. P. Simpson. The Southern Railroad renamed the station to Celriver, South Carolina, after the Celriver Plant of the Celanese Corporation of America, which built its gigantic plant at this place in 1946.

Mr. Charles L. Cobb (1883-1953) was instrumental in bringing the Rock Hill Printing and Finishing Company (Bleachery) and Celanese Corporation to Rock Hill. The Bleachery began operation in 1930 and Celanese (Celriver) began operation in 1948. Mr. Cobb was described in Rock Hill as a "one-man industrial go-getter."

In 1946, Celanese bought 1,100 acres of land, the former Carhartt Plantation site, along the Catawba River. Celanese decided to have the plantation buildings dismantled and buried in 1952 because of "vandalism and immoral acts." Matthews & Benfield Excavation Company was contracted to dismantle and bury the buildings. The massive work effort was a process over years rather than a "do-it-and-done" job.

Ronnie Parrish of Rock Hill worked for Matthews & Benfield Excavation Company during some of the years the buildings on the Carhartt Plantation were dismantled and buried. In several conversations with Ronnie, he said that the buildings were torn down in a series of moves rather than all at once. They were buried in a big gully on the west side of the Catawba River before you reached the railroad trestle. Two round concrete grape vats for processing wine were kept within the Rock Hill area. Ronnie humorously remembers that during the dismantling many people came to the work site looking for souvenirs from the mansion, houses, and other buildings.

Dave and Julia Moore were last to live in the house. According to the 1941-1942 Rock Hill City Directories, Mr. Moore lived on Route 3 and was the bookkeeper for Bass Furniture Store on Main Street in Rock Hill. The 1936 Rock Hill City Directory lists 241 East Main Street as their address. They later moved to Oxford, North Carolina.

Celanese sold the site of the former Carhartt Plantation in 2005 for $40 million to Pollution Risk Services of Cincinnati, a subsidiary of the Assured Group of Companies. The foundational remains of the Carhartt mansion and other buildings are now on developer's land, and they are rapidly developing the Riverwalk residential and business community.

York County Government Center
6 South Congress Street, York, South Carolina
Register of Deeds
1924   Plat Book 2, pages 574 (two pages), May 15
        Hamilton Carhartt and Hamilton Carhartt Mill No. 2
        Sold at Public Auction by the York County, Clerk of Court, T. E. Mackin
        Bought by: L. W. Weil and J. H. Weil, partners in L. W. Weil and Company.
        Advertised October 7, 1924, for $30,000
        All of that certain plantation or tract of land . . . 1,089 Acres +-
                Recorded: June 15, 1915, Book 32, page 330
                Deed Dated: January 9, 1917, Book 45, page 394
                Recorded: February 11, 1925

Rock Hill, <u>The Evening Herald</u>, October 7, 1924
CARHARTT FARM IS SOLD TODAY
The Hamilton Carhartt farm, bungalow and the site of the Catawba River Golf Club was purchased today by Dunlap & Dunlap, Rock Hill attorneys, agents for L. H. Weil & Company of Montgomery, Ala., for a consideration of $60,000, it was announced today.

The plantation is known over the entire state and is considered highly valuable. The Country Club has a lease on its site for four years, however. No plans for development have been announced.

York County Government Center
6 South Congress Street, York, South Carolina
<u>Register of Deeds</u>

1907	Carhartt began buying land and building plantation
1924	Carhartt Plantation sold to L. H. Weil & Company
1946	Plat Book 3, page 231, April 4 Weil Tract (Dunlap Tract, Bynum Tract, Moore Tract) sold to Celanese Corporation of America H. H. White C. E. Total Acres: 1,094.62 Original Carhartt Plantation
1946	L. H. Weil & Company sold to Celanese Corporation of America
2005	Celanese Corporation of America sold for $40 Million Dollars sold to Pollution Risk Services of Cincinnati, subsidiary of Assured Group of Companies Developing residential and businesses in community named Riverwalk

**The foundational remains of buildings on a bluff
are the tatters of Carhartt's dream.**

Located in back area of former Carhartt Plantation
(Mis-spelled Carhartt)

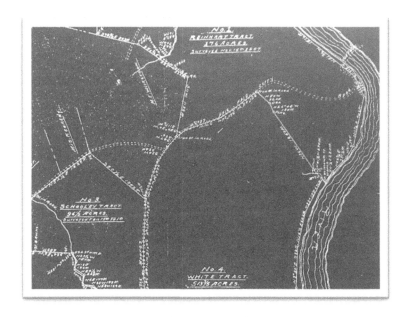

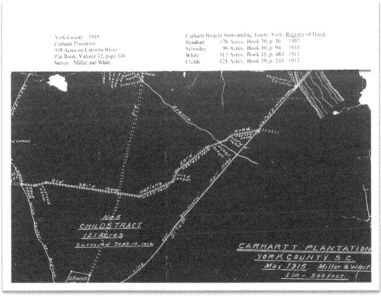

Carhartt bought all of the tracts of land
on this bluff of Catawba River

Nation Ford Trestle roofed in 1854
Burned on 19 April 1865 by Union forces under Major E. C. Moderwell
of the Twelfth Ohio Cavalry
Pictorial History of The Civil War, by T. Belknap, 1866
Courtesy of Mary B. Mallaney

CARHARTT'S ENGLISH VILLAGE

"The 'Carhartt Way' is to make denim better than any other.
The prosperity of my employees creates better denim."
Hamilton Carhartt

Round cottage in the English Village
Staff Photo, Rock Hill, <u>The Herald</u>

In 1916-1917, a time when outdoor privies, honey wagons (vehicles to collect and carry human waste), wells, and kerosene lamps were the accepted way of life and you swept your front yard with a hand-made straw broom, Hamilton Carhartt had a British architect design an English Village as housing for employees of Hamilton Carhartt Cotton Mills Number 2. The Village was decades beyond housing in Rock Hill. Additional housing for employees and staff was built on Red River Road. Some mill owners subtracted rent for housing from the employee's pay. Likely, Carhartt's houses were rent-free as long as residents remained employed at Carhartt's mill. Employees chose to remain employed. Carhartt's mill maintained a list of potential employees hoping for a job.

The English Village was located on Lynderboro Street, a hill near the mill. The area was called Carhartt Station or Carhartt, South Carolina. The English Village included the mill, 30 individually-designed artistic cottages (as described by Carhartt), community center with swimming pool, and a pond. The cottages were the first in the area to have hot and cold running water, electricity, indoor toilets, grassy lawns, and graded and curbed streets. The Catawba Power Company began operation in 1904 and provided an ample supply of electricity for the English Village and for the Carhartt Cotton Mills No. 2.

The 30-artistic cottages surrounded the community building. The outside of the houses was pebble dash or stucco. Some of the roofs appeared in pictures to be thatched. Standing in front of the last remaining cottage with its conical-rounded roof, half-round concrete porch, and cover is looking into the heart of art.

Vines hug the cottage in its final days.

You entered the cottage through a Cross and Bible door under an arched casing. The living room and dining room had fireplaces and mantels with extraordinarily beautiful windows across the fronts and sides offering a nearly-surround view of outdoors. The distinctive windows operated on the old pulley system, which was discontinued in the 1940s. The hexagonal front room was the showplace of the house. The rooms had deep-crown molding, overhead lighting with wall switches, plentiful floor outlets, and skeleton locks. Walls were lath and plaster, which was discontinued in the 1950s for drywall. Knob and tube wiring (the old cloth/fabric covered wires discontinued in the 1930s) was used throughout the house. Doors from the living room led into the dining room and into the kitchen.

Windows on fronts and sides of living room and dining room

The kitchen was standard with cabinets and a sink underneath a double window. The bedroom with good-sized windows had a closet when most people of that period hung their clothes on a nail behind the door or owned a chifforobe. The bathroom housed a tub, toilet, lavatory, and small hanging cabinet.

Every Friday night a social was held in the Community Center, providing an opportunity for the villagers to bond as a social family as well as fellow workers in the mill. Other events were held in the Community Center throughout the week including a night school for mill employees, homemaker classes for women, and a kindergarten.

In 1993, a Survey of Historical Places in York County determined that the round cottage could qualify for the National Register of Historic Places as stated by Sam Thomas, Director of Curatorial Services at the Museum of York County. No action was taken.

Hexagonal front room

Today, the land is undergoing development. Trees, bushes, and greenery have been clear-cut in readying for a new life by destroying the old. Rock Hill has lost a unique English Village. The outstanding architectural beauty and character of the 30 individually-designed cottages are gone. Once, it was a self-contained mill village with a waiting list of people who wanted to work in the mill and to live in the English Village.

Rock Hill, <u>The Evening Herald</u>, February 7, 1920
The article was about the happy and contented people living in the village. The thriving village was a scene of great daily activity and there was the making of a city at no far distant date. A model village was created and growing daily. A "splendid school" operated with Miss Carrie Bell Poag as principal and Miss Nell Wood as assistant teacher. Plans were in the making for a large, commodious boarding house that was much needed at the village. The mill was operating at capacity. The village proved little short of a revelation to many in Rock Hill. It was described as "the prettiest little village to be seen anywhere."

One can imagine the wonder and awe of an English Village with futuristic comforts in York County, South Carolina, with a population in 1920 of about 50,000. York County population exploded to 263,000 by 2020.

Chip Hutchison is Chair of Historic Rock Hill established in 1989 as a non-profit organization dedicated to historical preservation, education, and community. Chip contacted Strategic Capital Partners, developers of the former English Village site, for permission to make pictures of the last remaining cottage on the property. Chip then contacted <u>Luxpoint</u>, a company that offers 3D laser scanning, to measure both the outside and inside of the cottage. That information is stored on a flash drive. Historic Rock Hill is working with Winthrop University's History Department to use 3D printing technology to make a small model of the cottage. Our hope and dream for this project is to later create a full-sized replica of the round cottage to be located near the former Carhartt property, if possible. The cottage could be open to the public with a utilitarian purpose, perhaps as a visitor's center for the history of the Catawba River area or used as an educational tool in building methods of the early 1900s.

Prepared for the bulldozer. Razed in April 2021

**As with so much that man creates,
It simply fades away.**

Lynderboro Street

Over the years Carhartt's English Village became abandoned; cottages were vacant and eventually fell to rack-and-ruin. People up-to-no-good began to hang out there vandalizing the cottages, setting fire to some and even taking away the distinctive windows.

There was talk that Satanic rituals were being held on Lynderboro Street and the street became known as Demon's Trail. There is a cemetery at the end of the street that is now on private property and posted. It was said that people experienced paranormal phenomena of hearing voices and screams, begin pushed and scratched by an unseen force and capturing voices and sounds, strange orbs and mists on tape and film. A TV Paranormal Perception Crew is said to have captured these happenings on tape as well.

One of the cottages in the abandoned English Village was the location of a sexual assault in 2003 adding to the unsafe reputation of the English Village. A woman answered a newspaper ad for a housekeeper listed by a man who gave his name as John Helms. He took her to one of the cottages where the sexual assault happened.

Today, the area of Lynderboro Street has been clear-cut and redesigned for development.

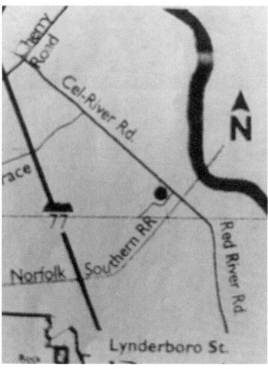

LAND TRANSACTIONS

"The Attitude of a Successful Businessman:
to spend 25 years in preparation, 25 years in application,
and then, if successful, 25 years in recreation."
Hamilton Carhartt

According to statements in area papers on 3 April 2001, 23 March 2003 and 10 July 2015, Hamilton Carhartt bought about 2,000 acres of land along Red River Road. Carhartt stated in a letter to the Washington D.C. Surgeon General in 1918 that he owned 1,400 acres of land along the Catawba River. He also owned the acreage of the Hamilton Carhartt Cotton Mills No.1 and the mill village off-of-then Trade Street in Rock Hill. With the accumulation of massive acreage and the often-spoken and written feelings of the peace of his planation on the Catawba River, it causes one to believe that he had plans before the Global Recession of 1920-1921 to have a permanent second home on the Catawba River.

Carhartt bought land in parcels and later the land was sold in parcels with the larger amount of 1,100 going first to L. W. Weil and Company, second to Celanese Corporation of American and third to Pollution Risk Services of Cincinnati. Today, the plantation site is a mixed residential and business development named Riverwalk.

Deed Books in the York County Government Center have a high number of pages listing land transaction of Hamilton Carhartt. Way-way too many to consider listing but here are a few of the land transactions during Hamilton Carhartt's years in Rock Hill. Other land holdings are mentioned in the Mill Chapter and the Plantation Chapter of this book.

York County Government Center
6 South congress Street, York
Register of Deeds

       Some land bought by Hamilton Carhartt Sr.

    1907   Book 30, page 36, 76 Acres
              C. E. Reinhardt Land
              Known as Mitchell Place. Bounded by May Wilkerson, White brothers, Isaac Jones and the Catawba River.

    1910   Book 30, page 94, February 10
              Schooley Home Place Tract
              Bounded by W. C. Biggers, Wilkerson, White, Wilson

    1911   Book 35, page 483
              W. E. White, et al., 513 Acres, 2 January
              Nations Ford Road, Old Moore's Ferry Road,
              Along water edge of River

1911   Book 36, page 362, $500
        Della Jolly
        South side of Hope Street
        Lot No. 53 on map of home place of A. E. Hutchison

1911   Book 36, page 421, Lot Rock Hill, 15 November
        James C. Witherspoon, Lot Rock Hill, $8,000
        Tract east side of White Street next to lot of W. N. Ashe
        Southern Railway and Catawba Real Estate

1915   Book 32, page 330
        Carhartt Farm 918 Acres on Catawba River

1923/4 Book 62, page 180, Tract Fort Mill Township
        $5.00 from Corinne Palms Carhartt to H. Carhartt Jr.
        Owned land East side of Catawba bordering lands of:
        Col. Leroy Springs, Dr. J. L. Spratt, Fred Nims,
        A. S. White, Old Nation Ford Road, Lee Armstrong,
        Dinkins Lot, Mrs. Orman, Dr. T. S. Kirkpatrick,
        Nation Ford railway bridge. C. W. F. Spencer, Trustee to
        Hamilton Carhartt Jr.

1946   Plat Book 3, pages 228-231, 4 April
        Celanese bought 1,094 acres from Weil Cotton company
        all of which originally belonged to Hamilton Carhartt.

Newspaper Listings of Land Transactions

Rock Hill, The Record, November 11, 1907
It is reported that Mr. Hamilton Carhartt has bought the Reinhart place on the Catawba River and will erect a fine winter home.

Rock Hill, The Record, March 22, 1909
Mr. W. L. Plexico, real estate dealer, sold to Mr. C. L. Cobb, Trustee, the Schooley Farm near the Carhartt Mill on the Catawba River containing 115 acres.
(Mr. C. L. Cobb handled land transactions for Mr. Carhartt.)

Fort Mill Times, February 23, 1911
$25,000 Farmland Transaction
During the last ten days J. Harvey White, Wm. Elliott White and Miss Emily White, sons, and daughter of the late Jas. W. White, sold to Hamilton Carhartt 513 acres of farmland, situated near Carhartt station between Fort Mill and Rock Hill, for which they received $25,000. The land was sold to Mr. Carhartt by Mr. J. H. McMurray for $50 per acre.

Fort Mill Times, May 30, 1912

Hamilton Carhartt, the millionaire overall manufacturer of Detroit, on Monday bought through the trust department of the Peoples National Bank, of Rock Hill, 200 acres of the Childs tract of land lying along the Southern railroad near its Catawba river bridge. The price paid per acre was $50. Mr. Carhartt now owns in the vicinity of the bridge something like 1,200 acres of land.

Fort Mill Times, August 1, 1918

Buys Brick Plant Land

Much gratification is felt and expressed here among all classes of citizens, but especially the business element, at the transfer of a tract of 506 acres of land held by Dr. J. L. Spratt cashier of the First National Bank, to Hamilton Carhartt, a part of the tract being that held formerly by the Charlotte Brick company. It is understood that the consideration was about $16,000. The tract lies to the southwest of Fort Mill and its nearest border is within a mile of the town. It is directly across Catawba River from the Hamilton Carhartt estate, a property which has received wonderful improvement since it came into the hands of the owner, having beautiful cottages, bungalows, walks and drives and a model cotton mill with cottages for the operatives which are supplied with all modern conveniences. In this mill blue denims are woven for the manufacture of overalls, and it is under the same management as the Hamilton Carhartt cotton mill of Rock Hill. The plans of Mr. Carhartt for the development of the land have not been disclosed but the businesspeople of Fort Mill are prepared to cooperate with him in its development and await with interest a decision as to his plans.

Rock Hill, The Record (Yorkville Enquirer), Monday, March 21, 1927, page 11

　　REAL ESTATE TRANSFERS, Ebenezer
　　Red River Cotton Mills to Josie S. Grant, 1 lot, full value.
　　Red River Cotton Mills to J. L. Grant, 1 lot, full value.
　　Red River Cotton Mills to J. C. P. Harris, 1 lot, full value.
　　Red River Cotton Mills to Lola V. Hunter, 1 lot, full value.
　　Red River Cotton Mills to Delia J. Hunter, 1 lot, full value.
　　Red River Cotton Mills to S. J. Hunter, 1 lot, full value.
　　Red River Cotton Mills to L. E. Hunter, 1 lot, full value.
　　Red River Cotton Mills to Annie Lee Harris, 1 lot, full value.
　　Red River Cotton Mills to Ida B. Faires, 1 lot, full value.
　　Red River Cotton Mills to R. A. Faires, 1 lot, full value.
　　Former property of Hamilton Carhartt Cotton Mills No. 2
　　until 1925 when sold to Red River Cotton Mills.

Hamilton Carhartt's years of buying and bettering land in Rock Hill had "only just begun" when the Global Recession of 1920-1921 hit the national and international manufacturing economy.

Carhartt's Land Ethic was one of community.
Improve the existing and preserve the natural beauty.

———————————

Index to Grantees
Book C, page 182
Some of the land transactions of Hamilton Carhartt Sr. and family.

Grantee	Grantor	Book	Page	Date	Recorded	Description
Hamilton Carhartt	C.E. Reinhardt et al	30	36	1907	1907	176A Catawba Tp $3,000
Hamilton Carhartt	A. A. Culp et al	35	94	1910	1910	115A Ebenezer Tp $3,150
Hamilton Carhartt	W. E. White et al.	35	483	1911	1911	513A Ebenezer Tp $25,680
Hamilton Carhartt Mfg.	Della Jolley	36	362	1911	1911	Lot, Rock Hill $500
Hamilton Carhartt	James C. Wither-spoon	36	421	1912	1912	Lot, Rock Hill $8,000
Hamilton Carhartt	C. L. Cobb	40	180	1912	1912	Lot, Rock Hill
(mfg.) H. Carhartt Cotton Mills		39	154	1912	1912	8A Rock Hill
Hamilton Carhartt	Edgar Jones	36	563	1912	1912	129A Catawba River $7,500
Hamilton Carhartt	Mary E. Childs	39	243	1912	1912	121A $6,050

Hamilton Carhartt	Jas. C. Witherspoon	45	116	1915	1916	214A Catawba River
Hamilton Carhartt	Mill Number 2	45	394	1917	1917	100A Catawba Tp
Hamilton Carhartt	J. L. Spratt	44	500	1918	1918	Tract, Fort Mill Tp $16,000
Hamilton Carhartt	Mill #2 Charter	44	813	1907	1920	Charter
H. Carhartt Jr	H. Carhartt Sr.	53	225	1920	1920	Tract near Rock Hill
Corrine Palm Carhartt	H. Carhartt	52	237	1921	1922	Tract, Fort Mill
H. Carhartt Jr.	C. W. F. Spencer Trustee	57	337	1922	1923	Tract, Fort Mill
Annette Carhartt	Hamilton Carhartt	54	390	1920	1923	Bill of Sale
H. Carhartt Jr.	H. Carhartt Sr.	54	390	1920	1923	Bill of Sale
Corinne P. Carhartt	H. Carhartt Jr.	62	180	1923	1924	Tract, Fort Mill Tp $5.00

*Bought land, grist mill and ferry in 1908 but was not recorded until 1912.

103

Index to Grantees
Book H, page 53
Some of the land transactions by Hamilton Carhartt Sr. and family.

Grantee	Grantor	Book	Page	Date	Description
H. C. Cotton Mills	J. E. Marshall	33	22	1908-1909	2 Lots, Rock Hill
H.C. Mfg.	H. C. Cotton Mills	39	154	1912	8 Acres, Rock Hill
H. C. Mfg.	Charter	39	427	1913	Charter
H. C. Cotton Mills	E. R. Partridge	44	409	1918	Lot, Rock Hill
H. C. Cotton Mills	Jno. R. Barron	47	49	1918	Lot, Rock Hill
H. C. Cotton Mills	Hamilton Carhartt	47	177	1918	Lot, Rock Hill
H. C. Cotton Mills	Catawba Real Estate Co.	48	505	1919-1920	Lot, Rock Hill
H. C. Cotton Mills	J. M. Cherry J. G. Anderson	51	360	1920	Lot, Rock Hill
H. C. Cotton Mills	L. F. Waldrop	51	17	1920	Lot, Rock Hill
H. C. Cotton Mills	Hamilton Carhartt	55	289	1921	Lot, Rock Hill

H. C. Cotton Mills	Hamilton Carhartt	57	148	1921-1922	Lot, Carhartt Station
H. C. Cotton Mills	Charter	54	392	1916-1923	Amendment to Charter
H. C. Cotton Mills	R. A. Childs Agent	54	798	1920	Indenture
Carhartt Overall Co.	E. L. Barnes	64	85	1921	Lot, Rock Hill

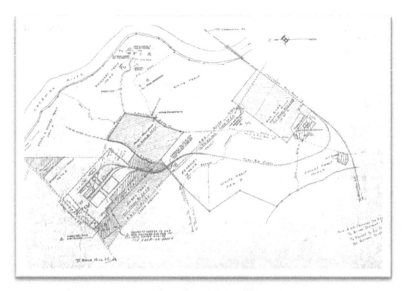

June 18, 1947. Celanese property showing
remaining Carhartt buildings in curve of Catawba River.
Survey plat Courtesy of Keistler Engineering Company Inc.

CARHARTT AFTER ROCK HILL

"My business of something over two million dollars annually,
built up almost in a night, is not the result of any 'gold brick' scheme,
but of good honest values, first, last and all the time."
Hamilton Carhartt

Hamilton Carhartt's final visit to Rock Hill was in 1925. After selling his massive land acres, mills, and plantation, he returned to his permanent home in Grosse Pointe Farms, Wayne County, Michigan. The United States City Directories list Rock Hill, South Carolina, as his permanent home in 1917-1920 and Detroit as his residence.

Carhartt's years in Rock Hill were of vast value to the city during the Progressive Era when founding families were attempting to make the city a better place. Rock Hill was changing from agriculture to an industrial environment, from rural to city. Carhartt provided jobs at top wages, the best of working conditions, housing, and opportunities for employees to develop skills in other areas. He employed local artisans and craft persons for his building programs increasing employment among those trades. He supported through financial resources the local groups who took care of the needy. He joined with Winthrop College to broaden educational opportunities. He worked jointly with other mill owners always supporting better working and living conditions for mill workers. His core values of safety first and the betterment of his employees were known statewide. Employees wanted to be a part of the Carhartt work family.

Despite the challenges posed by the 1920-1921 Global Recession and the 1929 Great Depression, Hamilton Carhartt and his sons, Hamilton Jr. and Wylie, managed to stay in business by closing all of their mills except Atlanta, Detroit, and Dallas. They survived until industry stabilized and Carhartt Clothing regained worldwide presence.

Hamilton and Annette Carhartt were involved in a car accident in 1937 at Grosse Pointe Farms, Wayne County, Michigan. Annette died that day and Hamilton died two days later from a fractured skull. Newspaper articles in early area papers tell of the accidental death of Hamilton and Annette Carhartt, then state that they were killed on the same corner where their daughter was killed earlier. This is a mis-statement and has been reprinted through the decades in other news articles. Hamilton and Annette had only one daughter, Margaret, who died in 1964. Their son, Wylie, and his second wife, Gretchen Stearns Yates Carhartt, were involved in an auto accident in 1933 and Gretchen was killed. It was Carhartt's *daughter-in-law* who was killed earlier in a car wreck and not his daughter. After the death of Gretchen and the serious injuries of their son Wylie, Hamilton and Annette moved into the home of Wylie at 385 University Street, Grosse Pointe. Likely, they moved there to help care for Wylie and his daughter Gretchen Welling Carhartt.

Carhartt's family followed his example and maintained the reputation of the best manufacturer of outdoor work clothing in the world. They expanded and broadened their clothing line from the blue-collar trades to outdoor wear and fashion wear with a new slogan:

"Born from Work,
Built for Play."

New clothing lines include the 'Back to the Land' campaign creating more of a stronghold than ever with farm and ranch workers; 'Works in Progress', a streetwear version of the Carhartt brand; clothing for women, children, and babies and flame-resistant clothing; fashion wear for the younger generation in skateboarding, hip hop BMX cycling, and others. Carhartt EMEA (Europe, Middle East, Africa) was formed in 2007 to provide workwear to the European Market. Carhartt Inc., itself, operates retail stores and allows certain other stores such as Tractor Supply Company to carry its brand. Carhartt has become a part of the local culture.

Today, Carhartt Inc. not only remains on the forefront of heavy- and light-duty work clothes but also has become iconic clothing in sportswear and streetwear. The clothing is top quality and affordable. Carhartt is still a private family-owned company in Wayne County, Michigan, owned by descendants of Founder, Hamilton Carhartt, with Carhartt's great-grandson, Mark Valade, as CEO.

Their core values are still the values and standards of their Founder, Hamilton Carhartt, who believed the way to manufacture the best products was through the prosperity of his employees.

Slogans of Carhartt Inc.:
Act like Hamilton Carhartt, be inspired by hardworking people.
Respect our past while walking bravely into the future.

**The best of our Past
is a road to follow
to create a better tomorrow.**

Learning from the Past

Hamilton Carhartt rode into Rock Hill on a train rather than a white horse; he left Rock Hill with a model of values and virtues in which we can all aspire. Carhartt was no ordinary man. He ticked all the boxes that embody the strongest set of moral standards for humanity, his fame and prestige did not influence the meaning or purpose of his life. His life offers insights into what life could be like when lived in the purest form. His code of conduct could serve as a template for us.

WORKS CITED
Preserving our Past

Bradford Jr., William R. Out of the Past. A History of Fort Mill, South Carolina.
Bradford Publishing Company, 1980

Brown, Douglas Summers. The Catawba Indians, The People of the River.
Columbia, South Carolina.
The University of South Carolina Press, 1966

Gettys, Paul M. Joseph Bartha, Horticulturist. August 13, 2019
https://www.rootsandrecall.com/york-county-sc/buildings/148-
ebenezer-avenue

Historical Center of York County, Culture and Heritage Museums
McCelvey Center, 212 East Jefferson Street, York, South Carolina
Pettus, M. Louise
Articles
Scoggins, Michael C.
A History of the Rock Hill Cotton Factory
The Rock Hill Cotton Factory Historical Marker Ceremony,
September 6, 2007
File Folder: Rock Hill Cotton Factory.
Map: York County 1910, Jones and Walker

Internet Source
Find A Grave

Keistler Engineering Company Inc.
Survey Plats of Carhartt Plantation Area
1947, June 18
Map of Property Celriver Plant
Drawing No.: 1379 dated 4-16-85
CCF E26A-52-22104
1950, April 5
Deed, BAM
1956, December 21
R. H. Marrett Reg. Surveyor
Reference of changes up to 1962
Referral Note: Precise property survey of plant site
drawn by W. C. White on 19 July 1946
1959, March 23
Aerial View PL-1W-132
1980, January 1.
J. R. Mosely

Willoughby, Lynn. The Good Town Does Well. Orangeburg, South Carolina.
Written in Stone Publisher, 2002 York County

York County Government Center. Congress Street, York, South Carolina
    Register of Deeds: Deeds, Plats

York County Library Main Branch, Black Street, Rock Hill, South Carolina
    Ancestry.com
    Newspapers on Microfiche:
        Fort Mill: Fort Mill Times
        Rock Hill: The Record, The Evening Herald,
            The Herald
        York: Yorkville Enquirer
    Rock Hill City Directories: 1908-1942, 1959

**As we grow Rock Hill,
Let us carry our past with us.
We are who we are
Because of Yesteryear's Leaders.**

APPENDIX

The Hamilton Carhartt Family
"Our business was not started to do the gainful thing alone,
but the just and honest thing, gainful if possible."
Hamilton Carhartt

Hamilton Carhartt Sr., Photo Courtesy of Gary Williams

Hamilton Brakeman Carhartt was born 27 August 1855 in Macedon Lock, New York, the son of George Washington Carhartt MD, physician-surgeon, (1820-1872), and Lefa Jane Wylie Carhartt (1830-1857), both born in New York. George and Lefa Jane were married in 1851. Lefa Jane was the daughter of William Dixon Wylie and Damarias Dalrymple Wylie. George Washington Carhartt was the son of Robert and Magdalen Mary Brakeman Carhartt.

111

George Washington Carhartt MD spelled his name with two t's.
BUSINESS CARDS – 1851
R. McClelland, Attorney at Law, Monroe, Michigan
G. W. Carhartt, M.D., Physician and Surgeon, Wayne,
Wayne County, Mich., Aug. 2
(Newspaper advertisement shown on Find a Grave site.)

The statement that Hamilton Carhartt added a second "t" to his name to differentiate himself from Carhart's who spelled their name with only one "t" is in error. Records show that Hamilton's father, George Washington Carhartt, spelled his name with two "t's."

Michigan Sudden Death
Special Dispatch to the <u>Detroit Free Press</u>, Jackson, April 21, 1872
Dr. George W. Carhart (sic) fell dead while eating supper at his residence about seven o'clock. He had been slightly sick with fever for the past 2 or 3 days. Heart disease is supposed to be the cause of his death. George is buried in Mount Evergreen Cemetery, Jackson County. Lefa Jane is buried in Soop-Pleasantview Cemetery, Wayne County, Michigan.

Civil War Draft Registration Records 1863-1865
Carhartt, George W. 40   Occupation: Doctor

Hamilton, "Ham" to family and friends, grew up in Michigan. At age 26 on 21 December 1881 in Jackson, Michigan, Hamilton married Annette (Nettie) W. Welling, age 21. Annette was born 18 December 1861 in Jackson County, Michigan, the daughter of Stephen Alling Welling (1830-1908), a business capitalist in Detroit, Michigan. In 1855 Stephen Welling married Emma Polar (1835-1912). Stephen and Emma had two daughters: Mary Welling born 1858 and Annette Welling (1861-1937). Parents of Stephen Welling were Asa A. Welling (1807-1854) and Cornelia Alling (1812-1888).

Hamilton Carhartt was educated in the public school system of Jackson, Michigan, and attended an Episcopal College in Racine, Wisconsin. In 1884, he began his career in wholesale furnishing business under the name of Hamilton Carhartt & Co. In 1889, he changed his line of operations to manufacturing working men's clothing and renamed his company Hamilton Carhartt Manufacturer Inc.

On 31 December 1898, Hamilton Brakeman Carhartt Sr. applied and was accepted as a member of the Sons of the American Revolution.

The Carhartt's second son Wylie and his wife Gretchen Stearns Yates Carhartt were involved in a car accident in 1933. Wylie was seriously injured, and Gretchen did not survive. In 1933, Hamilton and Annette Carhartt moved into Wylie's home; likely, to help care for their son and granddaughter Gretchen Welling Carhartt.

Newspaper Article:
Carhartts Hurt in Auto Wreck
James Standish also among victims
Members of three prominent Detroit families were injured in one of a series of traffic accidents that occurred over the weekend. One of them, Mrs. Gretchen Stearns Carhartt, was reported in grave condition in Charles Godwin Jennings Hospital as a result of a collision of the Carhartt automobile with a traffic signal post at the intersection of the Detroit Terminal Railroad and Mack Ave. early Sunday morning. She suffered a compound fracture of the skull and doctors said early Monday that her chances to recover were slight. Mrs. Carhartt, 35 years old, is the wife of Wylie W. Carhartt, 49, president of Hamilton Carhartt Overall Company, who incurred scalp lacerations. Their home is at 385 University Place, Grosse Pointe Village.

Obituary:
Mrs. Carhartt's Rites Tuesday
Death Follows Injury in Motor Crash
Funeral services for Mrs. Gretchen Stearns Carhartt, Grosse Pointe society matron, who died Monday morning of injuries suffered when her husband's automobile struck a concrete railroad warning post, will be held at 2:30 p.m. Tuesday at the William R. Hamilton Funeral Chapel, 2975 Cass Ave. James D. Standish Jr., prominent amateur golfer, who suffered a double fracture of the left leg in the accident, will attend the funeral as an honorary pallbearer despite his injuries, it was announced Monday. It was doubtful, however, whether her husband, Wylie W. Carhartt, wealthy overall manufacturer, would be able to leave Charles Godwin Jennings Hospital where he is under treatment for shock and severe lacerations. Pallbearers are selected. Other pallbearers, active and honorary, were announced as follows: C. A. Dean Jr., C. G. Waldo Jr., Falconer O'Brien, E. B. Caulkins, Charles Wright Jr., John M. Bloom, Paul Weadock, C. T. Thenevert, Robert F. Dwyer, Walter B. Ford, Frederick C. Ford, K. B. Alexander, T. J. Boquett, George R. Cooke, M. O. Williams, E. G. Hotchkiss, and J. W. Broadhead, all prominent in Detroit business and social circles. Services will be conducted by the Rev. Francis B. Creamer, pastor of Christ Church, Grosse Point Village, of which Mrs. Carhartt was a member. Burial will be in Woodmere Cemetery.

Police Investigate Crash. The police investigation of the accident, which occurred late Saturday night, had not been completed Monday. Inspector Henry J. Garvin, of the Accident Investigation Bureau, questioned five witnesses, who said that the Carhartt car swerved, apparently as a result of hitting a rough spot in the pavement just as it approached this concrete post at Mack Ave. and the Detroit Terminal Railroad. Mr. Carhartt was driving. Inspector Garvin said he would not question victims of the accident until Tuesday. Carhartt, Standish, and Mrs. Lee O'Brien with Mrs. Carhartt were in the automobile when the crash came. Mrs. O'Brien suffered a fracture of the left leg and serious bruises. All three were still in the Jennings Hospital Monday, although physicians said it was likely that Standish and Mrs. O'Brien would be removed to their homes sometime in the evening.

Newspaper articles in early area papers mention the accidental death of Hamilton and Annette Carhartt in 1937, then state that they were killed on the same corner where their daughter was killed earlier. This is incorrect and has been reprinted through the decades in other news articles. Hamilton and Annette Carhartt had only one daughter, Margaret, who died in 1964. Their son, Wylie, and his second wife, Gretchen Stearns Yates Carhartt, were involved in an auto accident in 1933 and Gretchen was killed.

Hamilton Carhartt's *daughter-in-law* was killed earlier in a car wreck and not his daughter.

Hamilton and Annette Carhartt were involved in a car accident on 10 May 1937 at Grosse Pointe Farms, Wayne County, Michigan. Annette died that day and Hamilton died on 12 May 1937 from a fractured skull received in the automobile collision. They were living at 385 University Street, Grosse Pointe, Michigan, at the time of the accident. Hamilton Carhartt's <u>Death Certificate</u>: 284-407 Wayne County, Michigan.

Detroit, Michigan, <u>Ashland Daily Independent</u>, 13 May 1937
Mrs. Carhartt Dies in Crash, Boy Driver Collides with Overall Manufacturer
Investigators of an automobile collision fatal to Mrs. Annette Welling Carhartt, wife of the overall manufacturer, planned today to question her husband, Hamilton Carhartt Sr., if his own serious injuries permit. Mrs. Carhartt, 77, was dead on admission to Cottage Hospital at Grosse Pointe Farms after the collision late Monday in which the Carhartt car, driven by a chauffeur, crashed with the machine of Edward Snethkamp Jr., 16, of Grosse Pointe Park. Severe head injuries were suffered by Carhartt, 82, while the chauffeur, John Pickett, 26, suffered bruises and Snethkamp escaped unharmed. The collision occurred as the Carhartts were on their way to return their granddaughter, Gretchen Welling Carhartt, 12, from school. Investigating with Grosse Pointe police, Assistant Prosecutor Harry Letzer ordered Snethkamp, son of a prominent family, held for investigation of negligent homicide. Snethkamp's father heads the Snethkamp Auto Sales Inc. Four years ago, a son of the Carhartts, Wylie, suffered serious injuries and his wife, Gretchen Stearns Carhartt, was killed in an automobile accident.

Detroit, Michigan, <u>Ashland Daily Independent</u>, 13 May 1937
Carhartt Dies of Auto Hurts, Will Be Buried with Wife Thursday
Hamilton Carhartt, founder of the overall manufacturing firm bearing his name, died at 1:50 p.m. Wednesday in Grosse Pointe Cottage Hospital of injuries received Monday in an automobile collision that took the life of his wife, Mrs. Annette Welling Carhartt. Carhartt was 82 years old and Mrs. Carhartt 77. Double funeral services for the couple will be held Thursday. Meanwhile police were searching Wednesday for additional witnesses to the fatal crash, which occurred at St. Paul Ave. and University Place, Grosse Pointe. Statements so far obtained from witnesses divide the blame between John Pickett, the Carhartt chauffeur, and sixteen-year-old Edward H. Snethkamp, of 630 Lakepointe Ave., Grosse Pointe Park, driver of the other car. Pickett was hurt slightly, and the youth escaped injury. The crash, which occurred at 2:30 p.m., took place only a short distance from the home of Wylie Welling Carhartt, of 385 University Place, Grosse Pointe, a son with whom the Carhartt's had lived

114

since 1933. The double funeral for Mr. and Mrs. Carhartt will be held at 11 a.m. Thursday in the home of a daughter, Mrs. Harold D. Baker, at 3198 Lincoln Road, Grosse Pointe. Burial will be in Woodlawn (Woodmere) Cemetery. Services for Mrs. Carhartt were to have been held in Mrs. Baker's home at 2:00 p.m. Wednesday, less than an hour after death came to her husband. The plans were quickly altered, however. Besides Mrs. Baker and the son with whom they lived, the Carhartts are survived by another son, Hamilton Jr. of Carhartt, Kentucky, a granddaughter, Gretchen Welling Carhartt, and Mrs. Carhartt's sister, Miss Mary Welling of the Pasadena Apartments.

Children of Hamilton and Annette Welling Carhartt:
1. Hamilton Brakeman Carhartt Jr.   1883-1961
2. Wylie Welling Carhartt   1885-1959
3. Margaret Welling Carhartt Baker   1886-1964

1. Hamilton Brakeman Carhartt Jr.
    Hamilton was born 18 October 1883 in Michigan. He married Corinne Marie Palms born 10 September 1884. They lived in Michigan, California, and Kentucky. Hamilton Jr. died 25 November 1961 in Los Angeles, California. Corrine died in 1973. Both are buried in Resurrection Catholic Cemetery, Montebello, Los Angeles, California.

    Obituary:
    Clothing Firm Vice-President Carhartt Dies
    Hamilton Carhartt Jr., 79, vice-president of the Carhartt Manufacturing Co., makers of overalls and one of the nation's largest makers of military uniforms during World War II, died Saturday. He lived at 445 Bellefontaine St., Pasadena. Leaves Widow. Mr. Carhartt moved to Pasadena in 1921 from Irvin, Ky., to establish a West Coast factory for the clothing firm. He held silver mine properties in California and Utah at the time of his death. Mr. Carhartt leaves his widow, Corinne P.; two sons, John P. and Thomas; a daughter, Mrs. Corinna C. Abel; a sister and six grandchildren. Funeral services will be conducted at 10 a.m. Tuesday at the family residence, under direction of the Wendell P. Cabot & Sons Funeral Home, Pasadena. Interment will follow in Resurrection Cemetery, South San Gabriel.

    Grave Marker:
    Resurrection Catholic Cemetery
    Montebello, Los Angeles, California
    Carhartt
    Hamilton Jr.   Corinne P.
    1883-1961   1884-1973

    Children of Hamilton Jr. and Corinne Palms Carhartt:
    a. Hamilton Peter Carhartt III   1909-1959
    b John Palms Carhartt   1912-1990
    c. Thomas Palms Carhartt   1916-1997
    d. M. Corinne Palms Carhartt Abell 1921-2016

a.　　　Hamilton Peter Carhartt III
Peter was born 27 September 1909. He died 28 June 1959 and is buried at
Resurrection Catholic Cemetery, Montebello, Los Angeles, California.

> Grave Marker:
> Resurrection Catholic Cemetery
> Montebello, Los Angeles, California
> Peter Carhartt III
> Michigan
> CPL 846 SIG SC PHOTO BN WII

b.　　　John Palms Carhartt
John was born 14 October 1912 in Wayne County, Michigan. He married
Ellanore (Corella) Scott Van Riper born 6 November 1922 in Saint Louis,
Missouri. Corella died 24 February 1995 and is buried in San Gabriel
Cemetery, Los Angeles, California. On 8 November 1969, John second
married Marion Kellogg (1902-1991). John died 12 August 1990. John and
Marion are both buried in Oak Hill Cemetery, Ballard, Santa Barbara
County, California.

> World War II Draft Card
> John Palms Carhartt　　　　10-14-12
> Born in Detroit, mother:　　Mrs. Hamilton Carhartt (Jr.)

> Grave Marker:
> Oak Hill Cemetery, Santa Barbara County, California
> John P. Carhartt
> U.S. Army, World War II
> Oct 14, 1912 – Aug 12, 1990

> Grave Marker:
> San Gabriel Cemetery, Los Angeles, California
> Beloved Mother
> Corella Carhartt
> 1922-1995

> Children of John Palms and Corella Carhartt:
> (1) Mary Shelley Carhartt Granieri　　1946-
> (2) Annette Liggett Carhartt Brandin1948-
> (3) John Palms (Jake) Carhartt Jr.　　1950-1980
> (4) Mitchell Scott Carhartt　　　　　1953-

(1)　　　Mary Shelley Carhartt
Shelley was born 22 February 1946. She married Robert Michael Granieri
on 17 June 1967.

(2)   Annette Liggett Carhartt
        Annette was born 31 March 1948. On 7 February 1969 she married Edgar
        Gary Brandin.

(3)   John Palms (Jake) Carhartt Jr.

        Carhartt Obituary:
        John Palms Carhartt Jr., age 29 years, died in his sleep, January 25, 1980. A
        native of Pasadena, he resided in Santa Barbara and is survived by two
        children, Jeremy and Joanna; and his mother, Corella Van Riper Carhartt;
        his father, John Palms Carhartt; sisters, Shelley Granieri and Annette
        Brandin; and his brother, Mitchell Scott; also, nieces and nephews.
        Graveside services and internment, 2:00 p.m., Tuesday, San Gabriel
        Cemetery. Turner and Stevens, Pasadena, directors.

                        Grave Marker:
            San Gabriel Cemetery, Los Angeles, California
                        Devoted Father
                        John Palms Carhartt Jr.
                        1950-1980

(4)   Mitchell Scott Carhartt
        Mitchell was born 29 March 1953. On 27 November 1982, he married
        Brooke Byrd Phillips.

c.   Thomas Palms Carhartt
        Thomas was born 21 September 1916 in Michigan. Thomas married Argil
        born 13 March 1914. He served in the Navy. He died 17 January 1997. Argil
        died October 2002. Both are buried at David's Cemetery, Montgomery
        County, Ohio.

d.   Marie Corinne (Coco) Palms Carhartt
        Corinne was born 7 May 1921. On 7 October 1950 in Los Angeles,
        California, she married Robert J. Abell (1914-1998). Corinne died 11
        January 2016. Both are buried in Chapel of Chimes Cemetery in Santa Rosa,
        California.

2.   Wylie Welling Carhartt
        Wylie was born 22 January 1885 in Grand Rapids, Michigan. On 7
        September 1907, Wylie married Isabel Patterson, daughter of Rebecca
        Musgrove Truby and Woodward Reynolds Patterson. Isabel was born 20
        August 1887 in Kittanning, Armstrong, Pennsylvania. Wylie and Isabel
        divorced 23 February 1924 in Wayne County, Michigan. Isabel died at age
        39 on 14 May 1927 in Manhattan, New York. She is buried in Kittanning
        Cemetery, Armstrong, Pennsylvania.

Detroit, Michigan, <u>Detroit Free Press</u>, 19 May 1927
Former Detroit Woman is Dead
Mrs. Isabel Patterson Carhartt, Heart Disease Victim. Mrs. Isabel Patterson Carhartt, formerly of Detroit, died suddenly in New York City on Saturday, May 14, of heart disease and was buried from her mother's residence on Tuesday, May 17. She is survived by two sons, Wylie W. Carhartt Jr. and James Neal Carhartt, her mother, Mrs. J. D. Birmingham of New York, and her brother S. P. Patterson of Pittsburgh.

Wylie second married Gretchen Lincoln Stearns Yates on 10 May 1924 in Detroit, Michigan. Wylie was 39 and Gretchen was 31. Gretchen was born 4 July 1892 in Detroit to William L. and Grace Stearns. Gretchen's first marriage was to Herbert Henry Yates (1892-1958). They had two daughters: Eugenie and Patricia Yates. Gretchen and Herbert Henry divorced about 1920. Gretchen died as the result of an automobile accident on 26 June 1933 in Detroit. Wylie died 4 May 1959 in Michigan. Wylie and Gretchen are buried in Woodmere Cemetery, Detroit, Michigan.

Grave Markers:
Woodmere Cemetery, Detroit, Michigan
Wylie W. Carhartt   Gretchen S. Carhartt
1885-1959   1892-1933

Wylie third married Margaret Ramsey Simmonds in March 1938 in New Orleans, Louisiana. Margaret was born 17 June 1895 in Knoxville, Tennessee, to Robert Hall and Eulah Carson Simmonds. After Wylie's death, Margaret married Paul Strasburg. Children: Paul Stephen Strasburg and Robert Strasburg. Margaret died at age 92 on 15 November 1987 in St. Clair Shores, Macomb, Michigan.

On Hamilton Carhartt's Sr. death in 1937, Wylie became president of the Carhartt Clothing Company. Wylie was instrumental in creating the outdoor-wear brand of Carhartt Clothing.

Detroit, Michigan, <u>Detroit Free Press</u>, 5 May 1959
Carhartt, Wylie W.
May 4, 1959, husband of Margaret S. Carhartt, father of James N. Carhartt, Mrs. Robert C. Valade, Mrs. Leverett Davis Jr., Mrs. Stephen Howard and the late Wylie W. Carhartt Jr.; brother of Mrs. Harold Baker and Hamilton Carhartt Jr. Funeral service at chapel of the Wm. R. Hamilton Co., 3975 Cass Ave., Wednesday, 11 a.m. Memorial tributes may be sent to the Heart Fund or Seeing Eye Dog Inc.

Children of Wylie and Isabel Patterson Carhartt:
a. James Neale Carhartt   1913-1961
b. Wylie Welling Carhartt Jr.   1919-1958
Children of Gretchen Lincoln Stearns and Herbert Henry Yates:
c. Eugenie Stearns Yates Carhartt Davis 1913-1993
d. Patricia Stearns Yates Carhartt Howard 1917-2012
Child of Wylie and Gretchen Stearns Carhartt:
e. Gretchen Welling Carhartt Valade 1925-

a.   James Neale Carhartt
       James was born in 1913 in Michigan. He died in 1961. He is buried in
       Kittanning Cemetery, Kittanning, Armstrong, Pennsylvania.

b.   Wylie Welling Carhartt Jr.
       Wylie was born 21 March 1919 in Detroit, Michigan. He died March 1958
       in Dade County, Florida.

c.   Eugenie Stearns Yates Carhartt
       Eugenie was born 31 December 1913 in Grosse Pointe, Michigan, the
       daughter of Gretchen Lincoln Stearns Yates and Herbert Henry Yates
       (1912-1892). Eugenie married David M. Whitney on 21 September 1933.
       They had two children. Eugenie and David divorced in 1938. Eugenie
       married Leverett Brainard Davis Sr. (1914-2014). Eugenie died 22
       December 1993. Leverett died 27 August 2014. Eugenie was cremated and
       her ashes scattered at sea. A plaque is in Saint Andrew's Memorial Garden,
       Lincoln County, Maine. Leverett is buried there.

d.   Patricia L. Stearns Yates Carhartt
       Patricia was born 22 May 1917 in Michigan, the daughter of Gretchen
       Lincoln Stearns Yates and Herbert Henry Yates. On 18 July 1935 in Grosse
       Pointe, Michigan, she married Bruce L. Beaudette (1915-1988) son of
       Oliver Leo and Verina Marjorie Palmer Beaudette. They had two sons:
       Bruce and Peter Beaudette. Patricia and Bruce divorced in 1944. On 15
       August 1952, Patricia married Stephen C. Howard. Patricia died 12
       December 2012 in Newcastle, Maine.

e.   Gretchen Welling Carhartt
       Gretchen was born about 1925 in Detroit, Michigan. On 18 September
       1948 at Grosse Pointe, Michigan, she married Robert Charles Valade (1926-
       1998) son of Cyril Kellogg Valade and Marion I. Anderson Valade. In 1959
       at the death of Wylie Welling Carhartt, Robert Charles Valade assumed
       leadership of the Carhartt Company. Gretchen was founder of Mack
       Avenue Records, the foundation Gretchen C. Valade Endowment for the
       Arts, and the Gretchen Valade Jazz Center. In 2007, Gretchen received the
       Max Fisher Award for Outstanding Philanthropist and is listed as one of
       100 Most Influential Women. She owns or owned two restaurants, Morning
       Glory, a coffee shop, and the Dirty Dog Jazz Café. She stated in an

interview that she could be found there five nights a week on a barstool enjoying the music

Obituary: Robert Charles Valade

Robert Charles Valade, born April 19, 1926, in Detroit; son of Dr. Cyril K. and Marian Anderson Valade; husband of Gretchen Carhartt Valade; brother of Sara Anne Gushee of Phoenix, Ariz. and Leatrice McKinley of Grosse Pts. Shores, Mich.; father of Gretchen Garth, Mark Valade and the late Christopher C. Valade; father-in-law of Molly Valade; grandfather of six: Byron, Catherine, Damon, Kyle, Gretchen and Cameron. Mr. Valade attended St. Paul's School and De La Salle High School, graduating from Grosse Pte. High School. He attended Miami University of Ohio and Michigan State University. Before he married, he worked for Royal Typewriter in Detroit. In 1949, he began working for Carhartt Inc., and in 1959 became Chairman, President, and CEO. In the 1960s, he was a member of United Nations business mission to Brazil through the Young Presidents Organization. He expanded Carhartt Inc. from a $2m company in 1960 to over $300m expected sales in 1998, with 3,000 employees. Mr. Valade was known and respected for his highly ethical business practices. His business achievements were many and earned Carhartt Inc. several awards, including the prestigious A.F.C./C.I.O. World Congress Labor/Management Award. He was a member of the Fiddlesticks Golf Club in Fort Myers and a member of the Country Club of Detroit and member and past president of the Detroit Racquet Club. Memorial Mass Thursday, April 2, 1998, at St. Paul on the Lake Church, 157 Lakeshore Drive, Grosse Pointe Farms, Mich. The family will receive friends one-half hour prior to service. Contributions to the American Cancer Society appreciated.

Children of Gretchen Carhartt and Robert Charles Valade:
(1) Gretchen Stearns Valade Garth. 1948-
(2) Christopher Carhartt Valade   1950-1986
(3) Mark Robert Valade   1953-

(1)   Gretchen Stearns Valade
Gretchen was born about 1948. She married Edward Floyd Garth on 4 February 1973 in Michigan. They had two children. They divorced in 1994.

(2)   Christopher Carhartt Valade
Christopher was born 26 November 1950 in Grosse Point, Michigan. He died 4 September 1986 in Carlton County, Minnesota.

(3)   Mark Robert Valade
Mark was born 21 June 1953. He became President of Carhartt Clothing in 1996.

120

3.   Margaret Welling Carhartt
Margaret was born 10 August 1886 in Detroit, Michigan. On 18 November 1908, Margaret married Harold Danforth Baker in Detroit, Michigan. Harold was born 22 September 1884. Harold died 3 March 1948. Margaret died 19 January 1964. Both are buried in Woodlawn Cemetery, Detroit, Michigan.

Obituary:
Mrs. Margaret Carhartt Baker
Services for Mrs. Baker, 76, lifelong Detroit area resident will be in her home 319 Lincoln, Grosse Pointe, at 11 a.m. Tuesday. Mrs. Baker died in her home Sunday. Burial will be in Woodlawn Cemetery. She was a member of the Country Club, Detroit Garden Club of Michigan, Detroit Junior League, and Christ Church in Grosse Pointe. Mrs. Baker, widow of Harold Dainforth Baker, is survived by four daughters, Mrs. Jonathan Fairchild Butler and Mrs. William Langstaff Crow II, both of Rye, NY, Mrs. Harry Stoll Leyman of Cincinnati and Mrs. John Henry French Jr. of Grosse Pointe Farms, 16 grandchildren and five great-grandchildren.

Children of Margaret and Harold Danforth Baker:
a. Margaret Annette Baker Torrey Butler 1909-1976
b. Katharine Baker French   1910-1999
c. Barbara Baker Crow   1912-2004
d. Margaret Carhartt Baker Leyman 1917-2009

a.   Margaret Annette Baker
Annette married William Ford Torrey (1911-1957). She second married Jonathen Fairchild Butler. Annette died 21 July 1976 and is buried in Green-Wood Cemetery, Brooklyn, New York.

Children:
(1) Annette B. Torrey Fraser
(2 William F. Torrey
(3) Emory M. Torrey

b.   Katharine Baker
Katharine was born 30 November 1910 in Ontario, Canada. On 15 September 1934, she married John Henry French Jr. (1911-1994). Katharine died 24 September 1999.

Children of Katharine and John Henry French:
(1)John Henry French III
(2) Danforth B. French
(3) Henry W. French

121

c.   Barbara Baker
        Barbara was born 27 July 1912 in Grosse Point, Michigan. On 14
        September 1936, she married William Langstaff Crow (1910-1996) son of
        Ralph and Ella McClanahan Crow. Barbara died 2 April 2004 in New
        London County, Connecticut. Barbara and William are buried in
        Woodlawn Cemetery, Bronx County, New York.

        Obituary: Barbara Baker Crow
        Barbara Baker Crow, 91 of Masons Island, Mystic, CT, formerly of Rye,
        NY, passed away Friday, April 2, 2004, at the Hillcrest Nursing Home, in
        Uncasville, CT. Barbara was born July 27, 1912, in Grosse Point, MI,
        daughter of Harold Danforth Baker and Margaret Carhartt Baker. She
        married William L. Crow, September 14, 1936. Barbara moved to Rye in
        1936 and resided with her husband on Pine Island, Bill's childhood home,
        until 1980 when they retired to Mason's Island, CT. Barbara was a
        champion squash player in her youth and an avid tennis player throughout
        her life. She had a brief career as a real estate agent and was a consummate
        interior decorator which she pursued professionally and with passion. She
        is survived by her five children: William L. Crow III, Margo C. Reis, Bonnie
        C. Shek, Barbara Crow, and Ella M. Crow; a sister, Margaret B. Leyman;
        and by seven grandchildren and one great-grandson. In addition to her
        husband William L. Crow who died in 1996, she was predeceased by two
        sisters, Katharine Baker French and Annette Baker Butler.

                Children of Barbara Baker and William Langstaff Crow:
                (1)   William L. Crow III
                (2)   Margo Crow Reis
                (3)   Bonnie Crow Shek
                (4)   Barbara Crow
                (5)   Ella M. Crow

d.   Margaret Carhartt Baker
        Margaret was born 15 December 1917 in Wayne County, Michigan. She
        married Harry Stoll Leyman Jr. born 30 January 1914 the son of Harry Stoll
        Leyman Sr. (1873-1954) and Eva Belle Peck Leyman (1883-1947). Harry
        died 7 February 1988. Margaret died 12 April 2009. Margaret and Harry are
        buried in Spring Grove Cemetery, Cincinnati, Hamilton County, Ohio.

                Children:
                (1) Harry Stoll Leyman III   1940-2006
                (2) Margaret Leyman McHenry
                (3) Ray B. Leyman
                (4) Katharine (Christy) Leyman Ross

(1)   Harry Stoll Leyman III
        Harry was born 16 September 1940. He died 25 February 2006 in
        Clearwater, Florida, and is buried in Spring Grove Cemetery, Hamilton
        County, Ohio.

Grave Marker:
Spring Grove Cemetery, Hamilton County, Ohio
Harry Stoll Leyman III
U. S. Army
Sept 16, 1940 – Feb 25, 2006

Hamilton Carhartt lived by traditional Family Values.
He extended those standards to his Business Family.
His descendants have carried his Core Values forward.

Woodmere Cemetery

The Woodmere Cemetery was organized on 8 July 1867 by a group of prominent Detroit businessmen who purchased approximately 250 acres to establish a rural cemetery for the city of Detroit. The cemetery was dedicated in July 1869.

Carhartt family members buried in Woodmere:

Hamilton Brakeman Carhartt Sr.	1855-1937
Annette (Nettie) Welling Carhartt	1860-1937
Wylie Welling Carhartt	1885-1959
Gretchen S. Stearns Carhartt	1892-1933

(From Ancestry.com, Find A Grave)

Find a Grave Memorial Numbers

Name	Cemetery	Memorial ID
ABELL		
Corinne Carhartt Abell	Chapel of Chimes, Santa Rosa, CA	186362134
Robert J. Abell	Chapel of Chimes, Santa Rosa, CA	186362124
BAKER		
Harold Danforth Baker	Woodlawn, MI	218463362
Margaret Carhartt Baker	Woodlawn, MI	220933925
BUTLER		
Annette Baker Butler	Greenwood, Brooklyn, NY	154270877
CARHARTT		
Annette Carhartt	Woodmere, Detroit, MI	62408894
Argil T. Carhartt	David's Cemetery, OH	9741855
Corella Carhartt	San Gabriel, CA	110025641
Corinne P. Carhartt	Resurrection Catholic, CA	179221300
Gretchen Stearns Carhartt	Woodmere, Detroit, MI	62408479
George Washington Carhartt	Mount Evergreen, MI	15056154
Hamilton Carhartt Jr.	Resurrection Catholic, CA	179221290
Hamilton Carhartt Sr.	Woodmere, Detroit, MI	15203591
Isabel P. Carhartt	Kittanning, Armstrong, PA	97400053
James Neale Carhartt	Kittanning, Armstrong, PA	97400138
John P. Carhartt	Oak Hill, Santa Barbara, CA	78712583
John Palms Carhartt Jr.	San Gabriel, CA	110128025
Lefa Jane Carhartt	Soop-Pleasantview, MI	62511522
Marion Kellogg Carhartt	Resurrection Catholic, CA	120098029
Peter Carhartt III	Resurrection Catholic, CA	179191013
Thomas P. Carhartt	David's Cemetery, OH	131834441
Wylie W. Carhartt	Woodmere, Detroit, MI	62408747
CROW		
Barbara Baker Crow	Woodlawn, Bronx, NY	180569171
William L. Crow	Woodlawn, Bronx, NY	180569041
DAVIS		
Eugene S. Y. C. Davis	Saint Andrew's, Lincoln, ME	143818970
Leverett B. Davis	Saint Andrew's, Lincoln, M	135422508
LEYMAN		
Harry Stoll Leyman Jr.	Spring Grove, Hamilton, OH	78983355
Harry Stoll Leyman III	Spring Grove, Hamilton, OH	78983356
Margaret B. Leyman	Spring Grove, Hamilton, OH	78983361

MR. CARHARTT.

Newspaper Articles Relating to Hamilton Carhartt

Researched Local Papers on Microfiche at York County Main Library, Black Street, Rock Hill.

Fort Mill:	Fort Mill Times
Rock Hill:	The Record, The Evening Herald
	The Herald
York:	The Yorkville Enquirer

Rock Hill, The Record, Monday, June 17, 1907
A NEW FACTOR FOR ROCK HILL
The Entry into Business Here of Hamilton Carhartt of Detroit
Will Mean Much for Rock Hill--"If"--

A new force for progress came into Rock Hill when Mr. Hamilton Carhartt, the Detroit millionaire, became the owner and sole proprietor of the Bellevue Mill, now designated as the "Hamilton Carhartt Cotton Mills."

The Record doubts if the people of Rock Hill yet fully realize the significance and great importance of this move upon the part of this Detroit "captain of industry." That he will be an important factor in the commercial activity of Rock Hill there can be little doubt, according to those who are familiar with Mr. Carhartt's plans for increasing his industrial investment here.

Mr. Carhartt, who is a millionaire many times over, is remarkable in many ways. He is the largest manufacturer of gloves and uniform overalls in the world and the products of his tremendous factories are used all over the world. He is a living, shining example of what advertising can do. His business now amounts to nearly $2,000,000 per year--yet has not a single salesman. He has always sold his goods, is selling them now, by a wise expenditure in printer's ink. His advertising bills run to $50,000 per year and the money pours into his coffers as a result.

Already Advertising Rock Hill.
Mr. Carhartt has only recently issued a handsomely printed booklet as "a testimonial to his friends of the Switchmen's Union of North America and his companions in industry." This little book contains a description of the river and lake outing he gave his employees and their families on the 24th of last month. The thing most of interest in this book to people here is the way Mr. Carhartt has advertised Rock Hill. The most conspicuous picture in the book is a large double page picture of the Detroit factory (which is certainly tremendous), and at the bottom of this double page appear these words in large type:
"Owner and sole proprietor of Hamilton Carhartt Cotton Mills,
Rock Hill, South Carolina.
Where the sweet Catawba flows and where the staple cotton grows."

Now, when one thinks that this book is being sent all over the world and to over 4,000 distributing agencies in this country alone, one can see how widely this is going to advertise Rock Hill. And this is just a starter for us, because Mr. Carhartt believes in advertising first, last and all the time and undoubtedly Rock Hill will always figure in all of his advertising.

What It Means for Rock Hill.
The Record has no desire to go into hysterics over the advent into Rock Hill of Mr. Carhartt's magic wand and we have no intention of being accused of printing "hot air," as the saying goes. But this paper has every reason for saying that the entry of Mr. Carhartt into Rock Hill will prove to be of vast value to our growing city.

It seems to be pretty certain that Mr. Carhartt will build a large factory here for the manufacture of his goods to supply his large Southern trade--this city, of course, to be the distributing point for that purpose. Again, it is understood that he will build a handsome inter home, either in this city or on the banks of the Catawba--which would certainly more intimately identify him with the life of Rock Hill.

Mr. Carhartt's Maxims. The giant corporation of which Mr. Carhartt is president is an 8-hour profit-sharing corporation. In other words, the employees are stockholders. His son, Hamilton, Jr., a young man under 30, is vice-president and general manager, and upon his shoulders now devolve the management of this immense business. This business was incorporated the first of the present year, and at that time he distributed absolutely to all of his employees who had been with him a certain time many thousands of dollars' worth of stock in the new company, earning 7 percent, and to all he gave the privilege of buying more stock at par, though on the open market the stock is way above par. Upon the incorporation of his business, he turned the entire management of it over to his son and then proceeded to the fulfilment of a resolution made by him when a boy viz: "To spend 25 years in preparation, 25 years in application, and then, if successful, 25 years in recreation." Mr. Carhartt has been wonderfully successful and has now entered upon the third "lap" of his career, that of enjoying the fortune he has made.

The Personality of the Man.
Mr. Carhartt is a man of charming personality, with the most beautiful manners, clearly marking him as a cultured man of the world. A banker in Detroit recently wrote to a gentleman in Rock Hill concerning him saying among other things: "He is a prince in every sense of the word, full of the chivalry of the South and the ginger of the North."

Now that seems to The Record to be a very pat and handsome appreciation of this man from his own hometown and a prophet who hath honor in his own country must be all right, sure enough. Mr. Carhartt enters largely into all the affairs of the beautiful city of Detroit, but he says he's on the retired list now, so far as his business there is concerned.

He Should be Held Fast.

Now, <u>The Record</u> believes that here is a man whom Rock Hill should hold fast with gripping irons of appreciation and conciliation. People here now readily realize and admit how it was that Rock Hill lost the opportunity of being selected headquarters for the immense business of that giant corporation, the Southern Power Company, then the Catawba Power Company, how they fought and antagonized "that New York crowd," until Dr. Gil Wylie retired in disgust and selected Charlotte as headquarters.

Let us not repeat these tactics with Mr. Carhartt. Rather should we welcome the gentleman with open arms. Rock Hill is too large a place to have her future placed in jeopardy by petty jealousies, by sectional fanaticism. There should be no North, nor South, no East, nor West. We should all work for the common good and the commercial aggrandizement of Rock Hill, in other words, "Push Rock Hill." And it is such men as Dr. Gil Wylie and this latest comer, Mr. Carhartt, who could help largely to place Rock Hill in the front ranks.

Rock Hill, The Record
Thursday, July 25, 1907

CARHARTT TO BUILD CLUBHOUSE

The Record some time ago printed an article with reference to the entry into Rock Hill of Mr. Hamilton Carhartt, the multi-millionaire of Detroit, Mich., and intimated at that time that great things might be expected from him, in one shape or another.

Mr. Carhartt is not only a very rich man, but he is a man who does things and he loses no time in getting his work started and pushed to a successful issue.

As will be remembered Mr. Carhartt is now the sole owner of the old Bellevue Mill No. 2 and it is for general betterment of the condition of the mill help that his activities are now being directed.

His first move in this direction will be the erection of a large and splendidly appointed club house for the use of the employees of the mill. This building, which will be of brick and three stories, will be erected on the corner of the mill lot, facing the passenger depot. Mr. Carhartt proposes to make this the finest building of its kind in the South. Plans are being drawn for it in Detroit and are said to be about completed and it is expected that work on the structure will very shortly be started.

The basement floor will contain two large swimming pools, one for men and the other for women. There will also be a number of shower baths, private baths, etc.

On the second floor will be a reading room for men, as well as one for the women. On this floor also will be a lecture room, a kindergarten, classrooms for night school, a sewing room and a cooking room, where competent instructors will be at all times.

The third floor will be used as an auditorium, with a stage and all the usual accessories.

The night school will be started within two weeks and for this purpose a cottage will be used until the main building is completed.

It is the policy of Mr. Carhartt and his local representatives to give the employees a full chance to develop their talents. Those who are musically inclined will be given proper opportunities. A brass band will be organized among the men and a stringed instrument orchestra among the women, and the instruments will all be furnished by Mr. Carhartt.

Not the least thing done by Mr. Carhartt was the choice by him of Miss ? Steele of this city as his secretary for this welfare work. She is a thoroughly capable woman entirely qualified for the work. For several years she has been doing work of this character in the mill section. She has but recently returned from Greenville, S.C., and Asheville, N.C., to get information at first hand relative to this work and later on will go to Detroit for a conference with Mr. Carhartt in order to be perfectly informed of the plans for the future. Miss Steele will be in complete charge of the work here and The Record will testify that Mr. Carhartt could have hunted far and wide and never made so good a choice.

It of course goes without saying that the mill people are thoroughly aroused . . . They have been allowed to contribute to the plan and they have done so liberally.

While this building is, of course, a large part of Mr. Carhartt's welfare plan, his energies are likewise being extended towards making the people more comfortable in their homes. He intends that the homes shall have modern conveniences and that the mill village shall be improved. Cement sidewalks will be laid throughout and running water and electric lights will be put in each house. Further improvements will be made to each house in the way of comfort and convenience as the employees show their appreciation of them.

The houses of the mill people will be furnished with potted plants and flowers, with stands for them, and their cultivation will be encouraged. Further, there will be built a large greenhouse on the lawn of the mill where the villagers may place their flowers in the winter.

What It All Means.
Some people may ask what all this means, whether there is not a selfish motive in it. The answer is, that the real issue, the arch stone of the whole proposition, is the perfection of the "Carhartt denim," to make it just a little better than any other. It's the "Carhartt Way" to make the betterment, the uplifting, the prosperity of his employees the lever by which this result is attained. It is so in Detroit. It will be so here. It is the truest kind of philanthropy.

The wonderful possibilities of a movement such as this can readily be seen. It will not only raise the status of the Carhartt employees, but will spur to like effort other manufacturers, and thus our entire city will be benefited.

The other mill managers in Rock Hill have already done a noble work on behalf of the welfare of their people, and The Record is proud of them.

131

Rock Hill, <u>The Record</u>
October 21, 1907

The reporter of <u>The Record</u> paid a visit one evening last week to the Carhartt Mill school, which is in charge of Miss Lois Steele, assisted by Miss Cammie Smith, and was very much surprised to find such an interesting work going on there, most especially under the conditions that exist and which only one who is on the grounds and familiar with can fully realize just what a great work it is. In Miss Steele's class were about twenty children ranging in age from 10 to 16. After working hard in the mills (a great number of them) all day they come to the evening school. To see how very much interested they seemed to be in trying to learn something, and how well, in so short a time, they had learned to read and spell, as they only have several hours each evening, and as stated above, after working hard all day in the mill, seemed indeed remarkable. One girl that the teacher stated had only been to school three evenings, and that when she first came did not know anything at all, was spelling the general small, short words with ease. Numbers of boys and girls quoted verse from the Bible and repeated the Commandments and the Lord's Prayer. In the morning they have kindergarten and primary work and at different times of the week have sewing and cooking classes.

As stated above, such work under the conditions is a very difficult one, as a great many of the mill people never stay very long at a place and by the time they get the children in the school, and they begin to learn then they are moved away. That seriously handicaps the work. But this excellent work that is being done by the Carhartt Mill owners is bound to produce most beneficial results, as there is a great number of good people who are employed in the mills who can appreciate these opportunities and will take advantage of them and remain in one place so they can be benefited by them. Then the mill owners and the people at large, too, can realize what a great work this is.

Mr. Carhartt is very fortunate to secure the services of Miss Steele to carry on this work. The great interest that she is taking in the work is immediately noticed in the conduct of the students as soon as you enter the school room.

It is work for which Miss Steele is peculiarly fitted and evidence of her skill are seen on every hand. She is the right woman in the right place, and as a consequence the welfare work there is moving along finely and is met with sincere appreciation by the mill people.

The Honor Roll

Following is the honor roll of the school:

Primary: Nellie Farrell, L. T. Farrell, Margaret Cauthen, Martin Robertson, L. J. Robertson, Floyd Hunter, Lawrence Hunter, Jasper Roach, Crawford Roach, Myrtle Ayers, Erwin Corothers, Thelma Arledge, Marie Anderson, Janie Anderson, Paul Sistar, Silas Sistar, Lonnie Sistar, Charlie Merritt, Emma Merritt, Annie Robertson, Carrie Robertson, John Robertson, LeeRoy Pressley, Josie Wright, Nellie Lay, Bob Deviny, Jack Brooks, Minnie Stewart, Georgia Melton, Marion Strait, Lester McCraven, Steve McCraven, Hattie McCraven, Arthur Estredge, Herbert Estredge, Purvis Doster.

Advanced Pupils: Ed Smith, Nina Flowers, Nellie Melton, David Boyd, James Boyd, Vernie Sistar, John Deviny, Lizzie Deviny, Otto Anderson, Mattie Anderson, Marshall West, Fred Strait, Charlie Strait, Lida Farrell, Clide Farrell, Irene Farrell, Emma McCraven, Bill McCraven, Walter McCraven, Ben Johnson, Huey Robertson, Vander Robertson, Davis Robertson, Bob Brooks, Walter Corothers, Edgar Corothers, Lester Corothers, Lillian Stewart, Ed Kimbrell, Walter Brooks.

Pupils from sewing class deserving special mention for neat work: Mrs. L. Flowers, Miss Mary West, Miss Mary Hunter, Nellie Melton, Otto and Mattie Anderson.

133

Fort Mill Times
January 30, 1908

Mr. Hamilton Carhartt, the millionaire overall manufacturer, who some time ago bought valuable cotton mill property in Rock Hill and later the Whitner farm on Catawba river, has now bought the Jones roller mill property on the river. The consideration is stated to have been in the neighborhood of $10,000. Mr. Carhartt will in the near future install electric generators in the mill of sufficient power to light that building and his handsome summer home on the Whitner place about a half mile down the river.

Fort Mill Times
February 23, 1911

$25,000 Farmland Transaction

During the last ten days J. Harvey White, Wm. Elliott White and Miss Emily White, sons and daughter of the late Jas. W. White, sold to Hamilton Carhartt 513 acres of farmland, situated near Carhartt station between Fort Mill and Rock Hill, for which they received $25,000. The land was sold to Mr. Carhartt by Mr. J. H. McMurray for $50 per acre.

Fort Mill Times
February 29, 1912

Make Overalls in Rock Hill.
The Carhartt Mill, at Rock Hill, will in the near future begin the making of overalls as a part of the mill's regular business. A cutter and foreman have been at the mill for several days, and hands are being taught to operate the overall machines installed recently. As soon as a sufficient number of the workmen become familiar, operations will begin and about sixty dozen overalls per day will be turned out.

As will be remembered, Mr. Carhartt, the overall manufacturer of Detroit, bought the Rock Hill mill several years ago for the manufacture of denim for use in his Detroit factory. He has made the mill, the village and everything connected with the mill models of their kind and in addition to this has built a handsome residence on his farm overlooking Catawba river, near Carhartt Station.

The Rock Hill overall mill will be run on the 8-hour union scale with union wages.

Fort Mill Times
May 30, 1912

Hamilton Carhartt, the millionaire overall manufacturer of Detroit, on Monday bought through the trust department of the Peoples National Bank of Rock Hill, 200 acres of the Childs tract of land lying along the Southern railroad near its Catawba river bridge. The price paid per acre was $50. Mr. Carhartt now owns in the vicinity of the bridge something like 1,200 acres of land.

CARHARTT COMPANY
INSTALLS DINING ROOM

The Atlanta Constitution of June 28 had the following, which will be of interest to Rock Hill people: That Hamilton Carhartt, manufacturer, maker for many years of overalls bearing his name, believes firmly in the proper consideration for his employees is attested by the sanitary, comfortable and economical arrangements with which he surrounds his employees, mostly young women, in the Atlanta branch of his factory, located at 75 1-2 S. Pryor Street.

The picture above shows a portion of the dining room of his Atlanta factory, caught at mealtime, when a number of his employees were partaking of their midday lunch. This dining room is the essence of cleanliness and is the most up to date in its arrangement. In it are large marble-topped tables, with imported, nobby chairs surrounding them. Everything is as spick and span as can be found in any café or eating house in the country. Behind the counter, ready to serve the girls, is an old fashioned, southern negro "mammy," who not only knows how to cook delightful dishes, but who knows how to serve and to do those many little things that are a delight to the feminine heart in a dining room.

And the greatest beauty about the Carhartt dining room is that no profit whatever is expected or desired from it. The employees are served most substantial and elegant dishes at exactly cost to the company. A dish of beans, potatoes, vegetables of all kinds, soups, pies, soft drinks, ice cream or whatever they like they pay only actual cost for it. All the employees are required to eat in this dining room, though it is entirely optional whether they purchase any article or not. Those who bring their lunch can eat it there in comfort, without the expenditure of a cent. If they like, they can augment it with a glass of tea or milk, if they choose. As the illustration shows the room is splendidly ventilated, and with electric fans in operation, the employees do not wait for a second invitation to dinner.

This company also carries in stock for its employees any number of small articles, such as face powders, handkerchiefs, hosiery, brushes, laces--in fact a big showcase full of those things which appeal to feminine fancy--and all sold at exactly cost to them. This sort of consideration for its employees puts the Carhartt factory in a position where labor is never an item of worry to it, but on the other hand it always has a waiting list and has in its employ now about 100 girls.

This factory was moved to Atlanta from Rock Hill, S.C., February 1. The parent factory is in Detroit, where Mr. Carhartt makes his home, six big branch factories being operated over the country.

E. L. Partridge, who was in charge of the plant at Rock Hill, is the resident manager.

136

A Man of Large Activities
The Record is in receipt of a booklet entitled Hamilton Carhartt Plantation, of which Mr. R. S. Poag is the very capable superintendent, and it shows Mr. Carhartt to be a man of very large activities. A map in this booklet discloses that Mr. Carhartt has overall factories at Liverpool, England; Toronto, Canada; Vancouver, B. C.; a wareroom at Winnipeg, Canada; also, factories at Dallas, Texas; Atlanta, Ga.; Detroit, Mich.; and Rock Hill. The plantation on the Catawba covers 1,200 acres and one of the chief features is "Houran," the Arabian stallion. Carhartt grows alfalfa, corn and cotton. He makes a specialty of breeding Arabian horses, Polo and Shetland ponies, Berkshire hogs, Shropshire sheep, Guernsey milch cattle, Hereford beef cattle, White Wyandotte and Rhode Island Red poultry, Japanese Silkies for pheasant egg hatching, pheasants for stocking game preserves, Carneaux pigeons, Belgian hares, Angora goats, imported white and domestic peafowls. Rock Hill, The Record.

Fort Mill Times
August 10, 1916

Carhartt Mill a Certainty
According to the Rock Hill Record, there is no longer any doubt of the purpose of Hamilton Carhartt to erect a cotton mill at Carhartt, three miles south of Fort Mill.

N. G. Walker, architect of Rock Hill, is preparing plans for the new mill. The mill will be three stories, with dye house, boiler rooms and two warehouses. Mr. Walker will have the plans for the first unit ready in two weeks, and there will be three units altogether. The first unit will contain 3,600 spindles, 200 looms and other complementary machinery.

The village at present will contain 30 houses, laid out in circular plan, a community house in the center. L. A. Pope, of Rock Hill, has been awarded the contract for the erection of two houses to be used by workmen on the mill.

The mill will be built of rubble stone foundation and piers, with brick panels, all openings to have large steel section sash. The building will be the most modern of its kind in the Carolinas. All the houses in the village will be of individual design and pebble dash outside. A complete water, sewerage and electric lighting system will be installed.

Rock Hill, <u>The Record</u>
March 26, 1917

HAMILTON CARHARTT OFFERS NEW MILL
AND VILLAGE TO GOVERNMENT

Hamilton Carhartt has tendered to the Government the use of his Mill No. 2 and all buildings and cottages located at Carhartt on the Southern Railway for any purposes of the Government service in the war emergency, a most patriotic offer. This new mill has recently been organized with the same officers who direct Mill No. 1. Following is the letter making a tender of the property:

Honorable Newton D. Baker
Secretary of War
Washington, D.C.

My Dear Mr. Secretary:

For nearly a year, we have been building new buildings at Carhartt on the Southern Railway four miles north of this city, twenty miles south of Charlotte, North Carolina.

These buildings we have been expecting to use when completed for the second Hamilton Carhartt Cotton Mills and adjacent to these mills we are building something like thirty artistic cottages on the side hill for the accommodation of our employees.

These buildings, which are rapidly nearing completion, will all have every convenience of water, heat, light and power and are most beautifully and delightfully situated at the foot of the Blue Ridge Mountains on the Catawba River.

Our president, who is with us now, wishes me to offer to you all of these buildings for any purpose whatsoever that you may care to use them for either as a base hospital or for the manufacture of munitions or clothing or cloth for the same or indeed anything that you may choose.

Notwithstanding that the machinery and tools have been bought and paid for to fully equip the buildings as Cotton Mills. We will gladly defer doing this, if you care to take advantage of this offer for any use whatsoever.

I have the honor to be
Yours most respectfully,
W. G. Henderson
Treasurer and General Manager

LIBERAL OFFER OF HAMILTON CARHARTT TO OUR GOVERNMENT
Offers His Plantation, and All it Contains, Free of All Cost.
The following letter will be read with interest here:

Rock Hill, South Carolina
March 8, 1918

Dr. William C. Gorgas
Surgeon General, U.S.A.
Washington, D.C.

Dear Sir:
The writer owns about 1,400 acres of beautiful rolling land, located at Carhartt Station on the Southern Railway, twenty miles south of Charlotte, N.C., and five miles north of Rock Hill, S.C., a map of which is attached. This land extends for three miles along the Catawba River in the foothills of the Blue Ridge Mountains.

Something like one-half of this property is under state of cultivation, and it has splendid outbuildings, farmhouses, tenant houses, dairy barn, mule barn, cattle barn, together with a herd of pure-blooded Guernsey cattle and seven saddle horses with full equipment for riding.

The writer has his own temporary home, or lodge, on an eminence over-looking the Catawba River. Nearby there is an extra cottage for visitors, and gardener's cottage. All of these are in a splendid state of repair and furnished throughout completely. Photographs enclosed.

The thought has occurred to me that Southern soldiers, invalided home from "over there," would much prefer to recuperate in the Southern atmosphere and environments, which are so dear to them, and I now propose to turn this entire property, with all of its buildings and belongings, to the United States Government, to be used as a hospital station, without any charge whatsoever for the same.

I will not only do this but will consider it a personal favor if you take this proposition under consideration, and, if possible, accept the same and in addition, I hereby tender you my personal service in any capacity that you can use me without any compensation whatsoever. If you deem it worthwhile, I will come to Washington at my own expense for an interview.

My own home, or lodge, can be used as headquarters for the officers and superintendent of the place, and extra buildings can be put up very easily for hospital wards, at locations that would be thought most desirable.

The plantation is well-supplied with water from an artesian well and from natural mineral springs, the waters of the latter having been analyzed and shown to be above reproach.

The buildings are all electric-lighted and there is an abundance of electric power furnished from an in-exhaustible supply from the Southern Power Company, one of whose great power stations is located nearby.

The land that is not under cultivation is heavily wooded with pine, cedar, juniper, maple, hickory and other woods and are intersected with foot and bridle paths throughout and all in all it seems to me that this would make a more desirable location for a hospital unit.

The writer also owns 2 cotton mills in the near vicinity of this property and if any of the maimed or crippled soldiers wanted to have employment, we would go out of our way to see that it was given them and we would freely give of our time and money to see that they were properly trained in the vocation of the cotton industry.

Trusting you will see and appreciate this offer, and that I may have the courtesy of an acknowledgment at your convenience, I am,

Yours very truly,
Hamilton Carhartt

Rock Hill, <u>The Record</u>
November 17, 1919

TO ENLARGE MILL VILLAGE
The mill village of Hamilton Carhartt Cotton Mill in this city will be greatly extended to meet the requirements of the new mill addition. The village layout and engineering work is being done by plans of E. S. Draper, landscape architect and city planner, Charlotte and New York City. N. G. Walker of Rock Hill is architect of houses and structures.

Rock Hill, The Herald
February 7, 1920
CARHARTT NEEDS NEW STATION BUILDING NOW

Happy and Contented Village Has Sprung Up Along Banks of the Catawba
Carhartt, Feb. 6. This thriving village is a scene of great daily activity and there is in the making a city at no far distant date, if one judges from the indications seen on every hand. One only needs to picture paved streets, the avenues already having been graded and curbed, to give on the prettiest little village to be seen anywhere.

The mill here is operating to capacity and there are scores of happy homes housing several hundred contented and industrious people. One great need felt by the residents is that of an adequate passenger station as they frequently desire to come to Rock Hill. The lonely little shed, that has for years served to protect one from the rain, while waiting for a train, is manfully doing duty at the same old stand, but in rainy weather the conditions are more disagreeable and there is no protection from the cold. It is to be hoped that the proper officials will at an early date take steps to see that a station, with telegraphic communication established, is erected here.

D. E. Mahaffey is superintendent of the mill and that he is right on the job is evident, after a trip through the big mill. And he has gathered together an able array of assistants, as follows: C. W. Ross, overseer of carding; W. S. Parker, overseer of weave room, with J. W. Davis, second hand; W F. Morton, overseer of spinning; C. A. Moss, machinist, R. R. Fry, overseer cloth room; J. R. Huddleston, overseer dye room. Mr. Green is head bookkeeper and postmaster. A small company store is being operated for the convenience of the people here and a new store is being built. W. M. Lybrand is manager of the store, with Miss Cora Nicholson as assistant.

A splendid school is already in operation with Miss Carrie Bell Poag as principal and Miss Nell Wood assistant teacher. There has been an average attendance of 45 this year and when the new school building, now nearing completion, is ready for occupancy the school facilities will be greatly increased.

Many new residences are going up on the village streets and the ring of the hammer and buzz of the saw can be heard from morn until night. Plans are also about ready for a large and commodious boarding house, and this will be another needed convenience.

Those who know Hamilton Carhartt are convinced that he will not stop short of one of the most modern villages to be found anywhere. The site is most ideal and right in the heart of huge cotton fields, just off the banks of the Catawba, where in years gone by the happy Catawbas fished and hunted, a model village has risen and is steadily being added to.

The growth of this village will doubtless prove little short of a revelation to many in Rock Hill and all are cordially invited to come out and get acquainted with their busy and prosperous neighbor.

Every Friday night a social is enjoyed by the villagers and these gatherings are proving a means of getting every person in the village acquainted. Last night the "party" was at the home of Rev. S. W. Whiteside and the occasion was for the benefit of the church and Sunday school. There were numerous boxes to be auctioned off and the proceeds amounted to $11, one of the boxes bringing in the neat sum of $4. Following the sale, the boxes were opened and the lunches enjoyed.

Rock Hill, The Evening Herald
October 2, 1925
BE PLACED IN MOTION VERY SOON
Deal Consummated at Stockholder's Meet Thursday

ENLARGE VILLAGE

Management Will Sell Elberton Plant (in Georgia); Retain Local
Hamilton Carhartt cotton mill unit No. 2, situated at Carhartt Station, four miles north of Rock Hill on Catawba River, has been sold to a corporation composed largely of local men. The deal was consummated yesterday at a meeting of stockholders following negotiations over a period of several weeks.

Announcement of the sale was made today by C. L. Cobb cashier of the Peoples National Bank and representative of the stockholders in the transaction.

The consideration for which the mill was sold was not made public. It is understood that the plant will be placed into operation within thirty to sixty days.

The corporation now in process of formation is to be headed by York Wilson and is to have cash capitalization of $150,000, it was learned.

Build Larger Village
It plans to erect about 30 additional houses and to inaugurate both day and night shifts. The mill will probably begin manufacturing white drills at least temporarily, it was stated. It has 8,104 spindles and 210 looms and will probably employ from 200 to 300 operative, it was stated.

In addition to the ideal village, a tract of 100 acres additional is included in the transaction.

The name of the new corporation or of the mill has not been decided upon as yet. York Wilson is to be president, it is understood. He is supported by other local mill interests as well as by New York capital, it was indicated.

Sell Elberton Plant (In Georgia)
The mill suspended operations more than a year ago and the village has been deserted except for watchmen and maintenance men. It was the newest of the Carhartt chain of mills but like other property of the overall magnate was taken into hands of receivers when the interests failed during the slump following the close of the World War.

The Carhartt management proposed to dispose of the large Elberton mill, at Elberton, Georgia, another unit of the Carhartt system, it was learned. The sale is to be at an early date. The Elberton mill has approximately 9,000 spindles. It has been idle for more than a year.

It is the purpose of the Carhartt management to retain the Carhartt Master Cloth Mill No.1, located in Rock Hill, it was also learned. The mill will continue to supply denim cloth to the overall mills in Atlanta, Ga., Dallas, Tex., Detroit, Mich., Liverpool, England, and Toronto, Canada, it was authoritatively stated. The entire output of the mill is being consumed and the mill would now be on full day and night schedule were it not for the power curtailment now in effect, it was stated.

C. L. Cobb will represent the Hamilton Carhartt cotton mills management in the negotiations for sale of the Elberton plant.

The sale of the mill here and the announcement of sale or retention of other units is the first definite information given out by the management since the system became deeply involved several years ago and went into hands of receivers.

———————————————

HERE IS THE STORY OF LODGE BUILT BY HAMILTON CARHARTT
By Bob Ward

> I laugh at the lore and pride of man
> At the Sophist schools and the learned clan,
> For what are they in their high conceit
> When man in the bush with God may meet

The lodge which Hamilton Carhartt loved more than any spot-on earth has been reclaimed from the encroaching weeds. The vines have been burned away; and the house is assuming again the appearance it offered when the wealthy manufacturer strolled its green walks in the cool of the evening and found peace there beside the river.

It stands on a slope overlooking a bend in the Catawba River to the right of the Rock Hill-to-Charlotte highway—a monument to a man who was one of Rock Hill's foremost adopted citizens.

Mr. and Mrs. D. B. Moore live in the home now, and they have begun to restore the grounds immediately surrounding it. During the lodge's long vacancy, the undergrowth crept up and encircled the buildings.

About the turn of the century, Mr. Carhartt built the lodge on the river as a place where he could find rest and relaxation from the responsibilities of operating his far-flung industrial chain. He set a heavy arched gate to mark the entrance to the estate. He built up the farmlands and imported fine horses and blooded stock. He fenced pastures with concrete posts—an unusual sight in this section. He built huge barns and stables and a caretaker's house.

Careful Work

But it was on the lodge itself that he called on workmen to show painstaking care. Hardwood and carefully chosen timbers went into the house. Wrought iron hinges and supports were used and expensive leaded panes were placed in the windows.

The lodge was built with an English "blow-way" through the center, a kind of hall open at both ends. The breezes from the river passed through this hall. In front of the lodge extends an open porch. When the house was built this porch commanded a view of the river, which may be reached by walks down the steep slope. Now the trees have grown tall and the waters may be seen only in glimpses between them.

The lodge was so constructed that when the doors and window shutters were closed no knobs or other projections could be seen outside the home. In constructing the guest house, next to the lodge proper, a small balcony was built around a tree to avoid cutting it down. The tree still grows upward through the floor of the balcony.

Bartha Has a Part

Joseph Bartha, a native of Austria-Hungary, who had been employed in the municipal parks of Bremen, Germany, was assigned the task of landscaping the property and setting out shrubbery and flowers. He worked for the Carhartt estate for 17 years.

Mr. Carhartt instituted the practice of flying the United States flag over his mill in Rock Hill (the present Cutter Manufacturing company). And when he built his river lodge, he had a tall flagpole erected and flew a flag from it every day. When the manufacturer wished to be alone with his family, he flew a white flag from this high staff and the gatekeeper far off at the entrance of the estate closed the gates, signifying that Mr. Carhartt was not at home to visitors.

Down the river from the lodge there was an island many older Rock Hillians will remember for it was a famous picnic spot of the day. A bridge led from the banks of the river to the island. Mr. Carhartt's friends came to the lodge to visit him and his guest book often showed the signatures of distinguished persons.

He became more and more attached to the wooded estate. Collecting selected poems, he published a book called The Old Plantation in which he expressed his feelings of contentment he found there.

New York Native

Hamilton Carhartt Sr. was born in Macedon Locks, NY and was educated in the public and military schools of Racine, Wisconsin. He began business in the wholesale firm of Welling and Carhartt in Grand Rapids in 1882 and moved to Detroit in 1884. There he established Hamilton Carhartt and Company, wholesale furnishings. In 1889 the firm name was changed to Hamilton Carhartt Manufacturing Company which specialized in men's working apparel. In 1915 the name was changed to Hamilton Carhartt Cotton Mills.

Meanwhile Mr. Carhartt had come to Rock Hill and purchased his first cotton mill here, now the Cutter Manufacturing Company. He spent many thousands of dollars in improving and beautifying the property. He built the Red River Mills, then known as Mill No. 2 at Carhartt Station. He also owned mills at Elberton, Georgia and Mobile, Alabama. All of them produced denim for his overall factories which were located in Michigan, Georgia, Texas, California, Canada and Liverpool, England.

In May 1937, Hamilton Carhartt and his wife were in an automobile accident near Detroit. Mr. Carhartt who was then 76 years of age, was fatally injured. His wife was killed outright, and he died two days later.

At the time of his death, he was president of the Hamilton Carhartt Overall Company with factories in Carhartt Park, Ky., Dallas, Texas, and Atlanta. He had two sons and a daughter. His sons were associated with him in business and at one time one of them built Carhartt automobiles in Detroit.

Mr. Carhartt was active in the civic life of Rock Hill and his influence was widely felt.

In his mills he placed placards which read, "Our business was not started to do the gainful thing alone, but the just and honest thing, gainful if possible."

Pride in Beautification

Mr. Carhartt took great pride in the beautification of his properties, and they were show places of Rock Hill. His improvement was not limited to his lodge and personal holdings. He did much to beautify his mill village and business sites.

As long as he lived, and for years after he left Rock Hill, he still thought of his lodge as "the most restful place he had ever seen." To him it signified a place of peace, a place where he could entertain his friends or be alone with the sound of the running water and the wind in the pines. He could forget the worries of his business interests, which extended from California to Liverpool.

Those who knew the late master of Carhartt lodge will tell you today, "He had an intense love of that place far beyond the ordinary pride of possession. To him it was more than a quiet woodland home, it was his retreat."

He included this verse in the front of his book about The Old Plantation.
O when I am safe in my sylvan home
I tread on the pride of Greece and Rome;
And when I am stretched beneath the pines,
Where the even star up brightly shines,
I laugh at the lore and pride of man.
At the Sophist schools and the learned clan.
For what are they in their high conceit
When man in the bush with God may meet?

————————————

NOTE:
Bob Ward worked for The Evening Herald as a reporter in the 1950s.

146

Rock Hill, <u>The Evening Herald</u>
August 7, 1959
RUINS REMINDER OF PAST ERA
By Elizabeth Reed
(First of Two Articles)

His name was Hamilton Carhartt. He was a Detroit multi-millionaire and there was a time, when he owned two Rock Hill area cotton mills, the present Gold Tex mill in Rock Hill and the Farmac mill at Red River.

He also owned a large farm holding on the Catawba.

Today, the ruins of his picturesque winter home near Rock Hill, on a bluff overlooking the Catawba River, are a vivid reminder of another era. The property now is owned by Celanese Corp. of America.

Except for the ruins, a yellowed book of poems, about the Catawba and a few faded pictures, there is little tangible evidence of Carhartt's years in York County. But old-timers remember him and their opinions of him are high.

Carhartt owned mills in York County at a time when outdoor privies and wells were the accepted thing for town homes and for cotton mills.

His dream was to provide running water, indoor plumbing, grassy lawns, shrubs, potted plants and other advantages for his employees.

His mill on the Catawba was to become a model, far ahead of other mills of its day.

The issue of the old Rock Hill <u>The Record</u> for June 17, 1907, tells of Carhartt's plans to buy Bellevue Mills.

Carhartt then was described as the "largest manufacturer of gloves and uniform overalls the world over, with an annual business of two million dollars, and advertising amounting to over $50,000 per year." <u>The Record</u> reported that Carhartt was going to build "a winter home either in the city or on the banks of the Catawba."

When he arrived, <u>The Record</u> had this estimate of Carhartt: "He is a man with the most beautiful manners, a prince in every sense of the word with all the chivalry of the South and all the ginger of the North."

A July 25, 1907, story tells of a dream which was never fully realized:

Carhartt planned a brick three-story recreation building on the banks of the Catawba. The first floor was to have swimming pools for both men and women. The second floor was to have lecture rooms, rooms for teaching cooking and sewing and school. All teachers were to be employed by Carhartt. The third floor was to have a large auditorium.

In 1912, Carhartt purchased 100 acres of land from the Child's estate in order to expand his manufacture of denim.

In 1913-1914 his second mill in York County was built by two Rock Hill contractors on a day-to-day basis. About the same type and architecture as the ones on his estate were erected on the property.

The mill was named Hamilton Carhartt Mill No. 2 and the goods made were shipped to Detroit where Carhartt operated butting and finishing plants. His slogan was "from the cotton boll to the overall," indicating that he spun his own yarns and wove it on his own looms.

In 1925 the property was sold to Red River Cotton Mills, which continued the manufacture of denims. Until the town of Red River was incorporated the name Carhartt Station was retained.

In 1944, the property was purchased by Harden Manufacturing Co. and since then has gone by the name Farmac Mills. But the name Hamilton Carhartt, in concrete above the mill entrance, is still there.

There are a number of persons in Rock Hill who knew Hamilton Carhartt well. One of these is Mrs. Bartha Talbert of State St., whose father was employed to look after the grounds at Mill No. 1. She recalls the winter home in its heyday, the bungalow, as the main house was called, the guest house where Hamilton Carhartt Jr. and his children later spent much time and a kitchen set off from the house.

———————————

A Past Era
CARHARTT HOLDINGS ONCE GREAT HERE
By: Elizabeth Reed (Second of Two Articles)

In time, Hamilton Carhartt's vision and Joseph Bartha's quiet skill made the former's winter home on the Catawba a fabulous place, a place of beauty, order, quiet and contentment.

Bartha, who died about two years ago, laid out all the walks, and outlined them with native stones. He built the porches around native trees.

He operated a regular nursery, utilizing whenever possible native growth and plants. Barbary hedges, Paul Scarlet roses, catalpa trees, a variety of cedars, were among his plantings.

Mrs. Bartha Talbert recalls the main house, the enormous living room with its massive stone chimney, which cost $10,000 to build, the open porch with its small native stones set in concrete for a floor and its five bedrooms. The house was erected by Frank Owens, a Rock Hill builder, now dead.

Time has not done as much damage to the tremendous bathroom as to other parts of the house.

Leo Nazareno Cullobosi, a young Italian artist, was employed to put in the imported ceramic tiles which formed the lavish bath, at least 15 by 20 feet in size.

The present Gold Tex, then known as Carhartt No. 1, was bought first and then the present Farmac Mill, known as Carhartt No. 2. Mrs. Ray at the Farmac office says that heavily set in the concrete above the doorway there are still the words, "Hamilton Carhartt."

One small tragedy marred their peaceful part-time life on the Catawba. A thief stole much of Mrs. Carhartt's jewelry.

When one leaves the Farmac mill grounds, which still retains plants put there by Bartha, one enters the Carhartt grounds by way of a tile covered arch, then down a long avenue of native cedars, still beautiful, to the gate. A silo and several other small buildings are still visible.

Lewis G. Harris announces with pride that he has sold the overalls, marked with a car superimposed on a heart, for about 60 years at Friedheims in Rock Hill.

Mrs. W. H. Hamilton of Saluda St. understands that Hamilton Carhartt went into the manufacturing of denim and the making of his product into work uniforms in this manner: In his early days he was a railroad engineer and being able to obtain no really satisfactory work clothes, Mrs. Carhartt made him some. He liked the cut and fit of her work clothes so much that eventually he had cutting rooms in Atlanta, Detroit, and other widely separated points.

Jerry Killingsworth Moore (Mrs. James S.) saw Carhartt just once. The caretaker had prepared quite a meal for a number of guests, but Carhartt was delayed in coming. He finally came and the meal was served. A very young Jerry thought she was feasting on turkey, but it turned out to be rooster. The turkey, which must have been a tough old gobbler, took longer to bake than the cook had thought.

Carhartt's sundial on the porch was so arranged that the north and south hands would not separate. He had the feeling that he did not want to express any regional differences.

There was a movie theater near the lodge for guests and employees, says Jerry. When Jerry came to Rock Hill in 1921 Carhartt had placed his property in the hands of a creditor's committee and the late Charlie Cobb was on the committee, a group of men in whom Carhartt had confidence.

C. A. Drennan Sr. of E. Black St. was a cotton grader and buyer for Carhartt during his time in Rock Hill. Now at Rock Hill Country Club, he was employed by the Rock Hill mills a total of 35 years beginning in 1918.

About 1907 Carhartt bought Mill No. 1 from Sam Friedheim and about 1909 he built the mill on the river known as Carhartt No. 2.

When reverses came upon the kindhearted citizen and lover of the lands on the Catawba, J. H. Cutter of Charlotte took over the Rock Hill mill about 1928. A Gastonia firm took over the mill on the river and Weill Cotton Co. took over the 1,100-farm stretching from the railroad trestle to the bridge. There, overseers Marvin Poag, Bob Poag and John Hayes were employed.

Mr. Drennan has heard that after they left Rock Hill, both Mr. and Mrs. Carhartt were killed in an automobile accident at Goose Corner in Detroit, where shortly before that time, his daughter had been killed while taking her children to school. He had made his last trip to Rock Hill about 1925.

"One of the finest men I ever knew." is the way Drennan sums up the man from Detroit. He understands that Hamilton Jr. is still operating part of the business, at least a sewing plant.

NOTE:
Charlie Reese was a paper boy when Hamilton Carhartt used to come into Rock Hill to catch a Pullman.

"He was a very friendly, heavy-set man, he would stop and talk to me when buying a paper. He was a striking sort of person," says Reese.

Mr. and Mrs. Dave Moore, later of Oxford, N.C., were last to live in the house. Vandalism and immoral use of the buildings made it necessary to dismantle them about 1952. They are now off limits to the public.

Hamilton Carhartt's love of Rock Hill, the Catawba and natural beauty is shown in the small booklet entitled "The Plantation," owned by Mrs. Talbert.

Here are the lead lines on some of the poems:
>   "Oh, when I am safe in my sylvan home,
>   I tread on the pride of Greece and Rome."
>
>   "I'm hungerin' to get away
>   Down yonder where the catfish play,
>   Down yonder where the skis are blue;
>   And every breeze that blows is true."
>
>   "Walking along the Catawba river
>   So peaceful in its flow,
>   Where the hills stand out forever
>   Quiet hills that thrill one so.
>   When I look, O soul and turning
>   See the Presence in the hills."
>
>   "Out of Carhartt's, where the corneaux pigeons fly
>   And the tiny Shetland ponies romp and play."
>
>   "You who stand upon the brim of the Catawba with history old."

NOTE:
Mrs. Bartha Talbert was the daughter of Joseph Bartha, horticulturist and estate manager of the Carhartt Plantation.

Rock Hill, <u>The Evening Herald</u>, March 11, 1982
Old Mill Progressive?
By Jane Clute

Rock Hill. Today it's considered progressive if a company has an in-house nursery for employees' children, but Claude Huddleston, 79, remembers when mothers brought their babies to Carhartt Mill with management's blessing some 60 years ago. Nursed the babies at the mill. "Kept them all day. I've heard my sister talking about women bringing babies to the mill, nursing them, putting them in a box to sleep and keeping them there."

Claude says he's not sure where the women went when they nursed, "but I can't remember them ever nursing right out in the open. I do remember women who had cooks (or maids). They'd bring the babies to the mill to be nursed and then they'd take them back home. And women who lived real close by would go home to nurse."

Older children stayed at home or went to school, though rarely for long. That was before the days of child labor laws, and back then you went to work when you were 11 or 12 somewhere along then. I went to work when I was 13 at Highland Park Mill.

Earlier stories in the Evening Herald about the old Rock Hill Cotton Factory (the state's first steam-powered cotton mill that began operating here in 1881) prompted Claude to dig through family papers and come up with a yellowed, dog-eared picture taken at the factory around 1910, maybe a little earlier. The factory changed hands and names many times over the years, and in the early 1900s was known as Carhartt Mills. Now the mill is owned by Ostrow and houses Plej's Textile Mill Outlet on Chatham Avenue. Claude says he is not in the picture he found. That was almost before my time, but my brother Howard is . . . Carhartt Mill, "and he was a grown man then." That picture, readers have said, was taken around 1920. Also, in the picture Claude found are his sisters, Lila and Etta and Etta's husband Walter Rayfield and Mr. Charlie Hailey. He was the bossman.

Work is no stranger to Claude, who took a part-time job delivering handbills for merchants when he was about 11. I had to walk all over town, I did it for 15 cents. He also worked as a "checkboy." You don't know what that is? He laughs. That was back yonder. If somebody bought something, the checkboy would take it up to the counter to get it wrapped and bring it back to the clerk who sold it. On Saturday I'd go to work at 12 o'clock and work til 9. I got 20 cents. He also sold the Evening Chronicle, a Charlotte paper, for 2 cents. I'd get half, a penny. Didn't sell too many papers, but I always had money.

Money was important to him, even as a youngster. Claude says when he was little, he could not wait to go to school but when I got old enough to go to school, I could not wait to go to work. I worried them to death till they let me out. I quit at 13.

Then he promptly hired on at Highland Park Mill. I swept floors and creeled (put spools of thread on warpers.) That was in 1916. I made 7 cents an hour. Later that year, Claude went to work creeling warpers at Carhartt for $1.35 a day. That was good money back then. I think we worked 11 hours a day and then on Saturday till dinnertime, but it was still good pay for kids. The bossman, Mr. Charlie Hailey, said he was making 60 cents an hour. Oh boy, that was money! Good gracious that was money! If we'd stop to talk a few minutes, a bunch of us would gather around, we'd say, "While we been talking, Mr. Charlie's done made 20 cents."

After getting fulltime jobs, Claude says, I could not wait to be 21, be a man on my own. Be independent. When I got 21, I wanted to get married. Things did not quite work out that way. He was 29 when he married his Faye. We got married in the Baptist parsonage down on White Street. Preacher Vipperman married us. Where did they go on their honeymoon? Claude considers a moment, laughs. Honeymoon. We didn't have any honeymoon back then. All we did was come on back home. My mother had a great big house and we lived with her.

When all of us children (there were seven of us) got married, we went home for a while and then we branched out. It wasn't like it is now. You couldn't afford to go out on your own at first. When I got married, I was working 65 hours a week at the Bleachery and making $13. You couldn't save any money, wasn't any to save. Claude says it's hard for younger people to imagine how much jobs and workplaces have changed. I made $13 a week and that's what I drew. They didn't take anything out of your paycheck, but there weren't any vacations, no paid holidays, no hospitalization, no unemployment. When you walked out of a place of business, you were on your own. If you broke your leg, too bad.

Many's the time, he says, when he'd stuff cloth in his shoes to pad the soles. After you stood on that concrete 11 or 12 or 13 hours a day, your feet would be killing you. It was rough. Yet, they always managed to get by, he says. When we got married, our grocery bill never was more than $1 or $2 unless you had to buy sugar and flour and lard and everything. And $3, good gracious, that was a sight.

Gardens helped stock the pantry, he says. And back then you didn't eat so much meat. If you wanted to buy meat, there wasn't but one place you could buy it, at the meat market. Grocery stores did not sell meat.

Luckily Claude says, he had no trouble getting jobs at various mills, even during the Depression. I've done a little bit of everything in my life, mill work, cabinet work, antiques. In 79 years, you do a lot of things. He and Faye, parents of three children, will celebrate their 50th anniversary in May. I considered it my lifetime job, Claude says. With a smile. You know, she's kinda wanting to have another wedding. I promised her I would go through with it, he adds, eyes twinkling. That was several years ago. I'll promise anything several years off.

———————

NOTE: Claude Huddleston (1903-1984)
York Observer, February 26, 1988
Tycoon In Overalls. Detroit Manufacturer Opened Rock Hill Cotton Mill To
Supply Denim For Carhartt Brand
Louise Pettus

In 1907, Hamilton Carhartt, a Detroit multi-millionaire who made his fortune manufacturing work overalls, came South seeking a factory that would serve as an addition to his growing denim empire. Carhartt was the largest manufacturer in the world of work overalls and gloves with a production that exceeded $2 million yearly. He found a cotton mill on White Street in Rock Hill that he was able to buy from Sam Friedheim. It was Rock Hill's oldest mill and the first steam-powered cotton mill in South Carolina. The mill had been incorporated in 1880 under the name Rock Hill Cotton Factory and opened in 1881 with A. E. Hutchison president. Friedheim had changed the name to Bellevue. Carhartt renamed the plant "Hamilton Carhartt Mill." He had other mills in Detroit, Atlanta, Dallas and Liverpool, England.

Carhartt built a winter home on the Catawba River. It was not long before he turned over the day-by-day management of his company to his son, Hamilton Carhartt Jr., and became a resident of York County.

In 1912-13, Carhartt built Hamilton Carhartt Mill No. 2 near the Catawba River on 100 acres he purchased from the Childs estate. He added more farmland until he had more than 2,000 acres. Carhartt's spectacular home on the Catawba River resembled a Swiss chalet done in stucco. Playing the role of gentleman-farmer, Carhartt set up Carhartt Farms with extensive dairy operations and a large number of Arabian horses. At Carhartt Station, Hamilton Carhartt Mill No. 2 employed more than 3,000 people. The homes in the mill village were of stucco and resembled scaled-down versions of Carhartt's personal resident.

The blue denim manufactured at Mill No. 2 was sent to Detroit where it was cut and finished. On the bib pocket of each pair of overalls there was sewn a small red heart with a representation of a car placed on the heart—thus, "car-heart."

According to the stories of the time, Carhartt was originally a railroad worker who was not satisfied with any work clothes then on the market. He told his wife what he wanted and she constructed a pair of overalls with a cut that he liked and with many more pockets than any work clothing then available. Carhartt liked his new overalls so much that he went into business manufacturing exact copies of his wife's work.

By 1920 Carhartt was spending most of his time on his model plantation on the Catawba River. That year he sent the following telegram to President Woodrow Wilson: "I wish to offer my home on the Catawba River, in the foothills of the Blue Ridge Mountains, with its complete equipment of servants, Arabian saddle horses, automobiles, etc., to President Wilson for his summer White House. It has ample accommodations for everybody." There was no reply.

A community house was built at Mill No. 1 in the summer of 1920. The three-story building boasted a reception hall, reading room, assembly hall, a kindergarten, first aid room, billiard and pool room and a 40-by-80-foot swimming pool.

Hamilton Carhartt was considered to be an "enlightened" mill owner. He had cooperated with Mary Frayser and Winthrop College since 1913 by donating mill property for child-care purposes, adult education and recreation programs.

The next year, 1921, was a hard year for cotton textile manufacturers. A post-war depression set in and Carhartt was overextended. He placed his Rock Hill mills in the hands of a creditors' committee. Charles Cobb, a Rock Hill banker, chaired the committee and attempted to sell the properties. Finally, Cobb sold the Carhartt property to Red River Mills. In 1928, J. H. Cutter of Charlotte took over the Rock Hill mill. A Gastonia mill purchased the mill at the river and Weill Cotton Company took over 1,000 acres of the farm, which stretched from the railroad trestle to the bridge (later Celanese Corporation property.

About this time, Mr. and Mrs. Carhartt were killed in an automobile accident in Detroit. It was at the same street corner that their daughter was killed while taking her children to school. The Carhartts had made their last trip to Rock Hill in 1925.

NOTE:
Later records have provided exact dates for some of these statements plus a more accurate account of the activities of Carhartt's years in Rock Hill.

Rock Hill, <u>The Herald</u>
Old Corn Merchant
By: Harper S. Gault
Special to the Herald

Some folks still remember Hamilton Carhartt.

Some of my readers suggested recently that we write something about the Carhartt mansion, which stood on a bluff overlooking the Catawba River north of Rock Hill on property that I believe now belongs to the Celanese people.

A bit of research turned up the fact that some three-quarters of a century ago a textile magnate from Detroit, Hamilton Carhartt operated two cotton mills in our area. He owned considerable land on the Catawba's banks and built a winter home overlooking the river that was a fabulous showplace then and for years to come.

I recall very faintly visiting the ruins of the old mansion many years ago. And as I remember, there was very little left to see by my visit there. Carhartt's name was borne by two cotton mills. One was in the heart of town at the corner of West White Street and Chatham Avenue. In later years it bore several names. The one after Carhartt was Cutter. Today it is Plej's Textile Mill Outlet at 115 Chatham Ave.

The other is at Red River, a settlement to the north of the city near the Celanese plant. It is Randolph Yarns Inc. and is owned by Gastonia, N.C., interests. But the name Hamilton Carhartt in concrete above the mill door remains there today.

Hamilton Carhartt's vision of a home on the banks of the Catawba became a reality through the skill of Joseph Bartha. The area became a place of beauty, order and quiet contentment. Bartha laid out the walks and outlined them with native stone. Porches were built around native trees. When possible native growth and plants were used in the landscaping. There were Paul Scarlet roses, catalpa trees and all types of cedars.

The main house had an enormous living room with a massive stone chimney. There were five bedrooms. There was a huge, lavish bathroom with imported ceramic titles. The bath was said to be something like 15 by 20 feet in size.

Carhartt was described as a man with all the chivalry of the South and the ginger of the North. Maybe that was why the sundial on his porch was arranged so that the north and south hands would not separate so that he was not expressing any regional differences. There were many other features of his home, including an archway leading to the home and a movie theater for guests and employees.

Early in life he was a railroad engineer. He was unable to get hold of any work clothes to his liking. Mrs. Carhartt made some for him and he liked the cut of her work, as well as the fit.

Eventually he had cutting shops in Detroit, Atlanta and widely separated places. And as time passed and he kept working, Carhartt was called the largest manufacturer of gloves and uniform overalls in the world.

His Carhartt overalls, marked with a car superimposed on a heart, were widely known and sold. Lewis G. "Rabbit" Harris, a late well-known Rock Hillian who was a friend of mine, used to remark with pride that he had sold Carhartt overalls about 60 years at Friedheim's Department Store, whose building still stands in Town Center Mall.

There was a story in an old paper dated about July 1907 that told of Carhartt's dream to make a better life for his employees. He came here at a time when outdoor privies and wells were common for town and country homes alike. He wanted indoor plumbing, recreational centers and swimming pools, lecture halls, rooms for instruction in household arts and other means for a better life.

Setbacks came upon this kind, far-seeing man and his dreams were never realized. He and his wife were killed in an auto accident in Detroit. He had made his last trip to Rock Hill about 1925.

I heard that Mr. and Mrs. Dave Moore were the last to live in the Carhartt home. I believe Dave Moore was connected with the former Bass Furniture Store on Main Street.

NOTE:
Harper S. Gault is listed in the Rock Hill City Directories of 1933-1934, 1936, 1940-1941 and 1942 as City Editor of the Herald Publishing Company. The 1959 Rock Hill City Directory lists Harper Gault as a manager at WRHI Radio Broadcasting Station. In the early 1990s he was the Herald Lifestyles Writer using a byline of "Old Corn Merchant."

The Charlotte Observer, March 30, 1992
By Lolo Pendergrast

RED RIVER. Farmers owe bib overalls to a Michigan Yankee who chiseled an English-style mill village from Red River. Catawba Indians trace a history of tribal trading from the paths worn into the community's rust-colored clay. Jefferson Davis can thank Red River's low waters for helping him run from a dogged Union Army. It's as if the flat-bottoms and crossings of Red River fill whole chapters of York County's history book. The history is written that the Catawba tribe and new settlers were drawn alike in search of a shortcut across the Catawba River called the Nation Ford.

The animals would find these places to cross as they migrated north and south, said Godfrey Nims, a history buff who works near the ford. The Indians followed the animals and hunted them, then used it to trade with other Indians north and south. Then the white man used it for trade. They'd drive cattle all the way to Philadelphia.

The community is bounded by Hoechst Celanese on the north, Springdale Road on the south and hemmed in by the Galleria and Fort Mill on the sides. Red River namesake is still uncertain. Some say it was named after Red River Cotton Mills and the nearby railroad stop of Red River, SC. Nims speculates it stems from clay farmland eroding into the waters.

The land hides the Great Western Trading Path, where caravans of Indians trekked to barter with southeastern tribes, the York County Historical Commission writes.

A historical plaque at Red River Road and the Norfolk-Southern crossing says you're probably standing on the path.

The trace is now so still that rail worker Bob Butts heard only the fizzle of the gunpowder he used to weld a spur track recently. It is quiet, he says. Sometimes it gets kind of boring.

Some believe Red River was a hub because of its trading crossroads and later its railroad, the Charlotte and S.C. Railroad, built in the 1850s.

It was a small town, says Mary Long, who researched Red River for a WNSC/ETV program. It had a hotel for travelers who were waiting for the water to go down so they could cross. They had a huge picnic when the train first crossed the trestle.

Historians say gray and blue troops waged the Battle of Stoneman's Raid at Nation Ford in April 1865, the dying days of the Civil War.

After one of the last Confederate cabinet meetings in Fort Mill, President Jefferson Davis fled through the ford at Red River to Georgia, according to accounts in the York County Library's Martha Bray Carson Memorial Collection.

The area blossomed in the early 1900s when Detroit textile magnate Hamilton Carhartt chose Red River as site of his Carhartt Mill No. 2. It is now Randolph Yarns.

Long's research shows Carhartt summoned an architect from England to carve an English-style village from the earth. Carhartt set up a mill somewhat resembling a castle. Beginning around 1909, his workers made denim for overalls, his invention as a young railroad worker.

On a rise behind the plant, Carhartt put up stucco cottages with conical roofs. He once planned to thatch them in the English village style, Long says.

On what is now Celanese property, he built a mansion and plantation with Arabian horses and lush gardens. I'll tell you where history is, says Zeb Carter, a Celanese engineering specialist, it's in places like this.

Carhartt so loved his house that he offered it to President Woodrow Wilson as a summer White House, Long says.

Carhartt's dream for the community was ambitions. On July 7, 1907, the Rock Hill Record reported Carhartt planned a three-story recreation complex with swimming pools, tennis courts, classrooms and nurseries. It was intended to be a model mill village and model plantation, says historian Louise Pettus.

Today, the plant is air-conditioned. Mill cottages are mostly boarded up and for rent. Carhartt Mansion is crumbling brick and slabs. But Carhartt left a historical note about his love for Red River in a booklet called "The Plantation."

> I'm hungerin' to get away
> Down yonder where the catfish play,
> Down yonder where the skies are blue;
> And every breeze that blows is true
> Walking along the Catawba River
> So peaceful in its flow,
> Where the hills stand out forever
> Quiet hills that thrill one so . . .
> You who stand upon the brim of the Catawba with history old.

COMMUNITY PROFILE:
Boundaries: U.S. 21 at Hoechst Celanese on the north, Springdale Road on the south, the Galleria on the west and Fort Mill town limits on the east. Historically speaking Red River is the home of:
>>The Nation Ford where Catawba Indians crossed the Catawba River to trade.
>>A cemetery dating to the 1800s.
>>The Carhartt Mansion, once offered to President Woodrow Wilson as a summer White House, the Carhartt Mill No.2 and an English-style mill village.

Quote: They said (the mansion) used to be one of the beautifulest places in York County, said 30-year resident Roy Swofford, 58, who lives near the old Carhartt Mansion.

Historical landmarks, 1652-1840
1. Great Western Trading Path.
2. The Nation Ford.
3. Historical Park at Red River Village 1960.
4. Southern Railway in 1960, laid as Charlotte and S. C. Railroad in 1852.
5. Randolph Yarns Mill at Red River Village in 1960 (bought in early 1900s and operated as Carhartt No. 2).
6. Modern road S-46-50 from Red River to U.S. 21 in 1960.
7. Nation Ford Road to Columbia, opened in 1823.
   County road linking S-46-50 in 1960.
8. The Crossroads.
9. Road from Herron's Ferry.
10. Nation Ford Road to Yorkville. Part of Eden Terrace, Rock Hill in 1960.
11. Old Saluda Road to Chesterville. Part of S. C. 72 Southern Bypass in 1960.

Landholdings in 1840:
The Rev. Archibald Whyte   William E. White
David Hutchison   Richard A. Springs
William C. Schooley

NOTE:
The Charlotte to South Carolina Railroad trestle over the Catawba River was destroyed on 19 March 1865 (10 days after Appomattox). General George Stoneman led his Cavalry Corps, including the 12th Ohio Cavalry, through the Carolinas with orders to destroy but not to fight. Brigadier General William Jackson Palmer was charged with the responsibility to destroy the railroads. Major Erastus Cratty Moderwell was ordered to burn the Nation Ford trestle. The trestle was burned from the east side (Fort Mill). Older men and boys were on the bluff overlooking the trestle with cannon attempting to save the trestle.

Hamilton Carhartt Cotton Mills No. 2 began operation after March 1917.

Historic mill at end of 90-year span in Rock Hill
Demolition began in mid-February at Randolph Yarns, built by Hamilton Carhartt between 1909 and 1912. Carhartt, a Detroit textile magnate at the turn of the century, is known for creating bib overalls. The building was purchased by the LaFar family of Gastonia, N.C., which ran Randolph Yarns until December. The mill and some houses Carhartt built behind it are listed as historical properties in York County. Photos by Andy Burris, The Herald

Demolition under way despite factory's rich past
By Sula Pettibon, The Herald

Rock Hill, built by the textile industry in the late 1800s, will lose a member of the family when the demolition of a 90-year-old mill off Celriver Road is completed later this month.

The demolition on the Hamilton Carhartt mill in north Rock Hill began in mid-February. Opinions vary on when the mill was built, but most say it was between 1909 and 1912.

Hamilton Carhartt, a Detroit-textile magnate who created bib overalls, built the mill and homes surrounding it. At one time, Carhartt also owned the Rock Hill Cotton Factory, the town's oldest.

The Celriver Road mill was purchased by D. R. LaFar Jr. and a partner in 1944. Later, it was named for an investor's son and became Randolph Yarns. It closed December 16.

The plant was just too old, said Adrienne LaFar, who sells yarn for Shelby, N.C., Four Leaf Textiles, who bought the assets. The equipment was old. We just couldn't compete.

The family thinks the 72 acres the red-brick mill sits on will sell better without the building. The mill and the homes are listed as historical properties in York County, said Sam Thomas, curator of history for the York County Culture and Heritage commission. Surveyors who compiled the list in 1992 said the mill and the homes could qualify for nomination to the National Register of Historic Places. The mill itself is a wonderful 20th century industrial complex. It has a wonderful facade, Thomas said. It would be quite a shame for this region to lose it.

Carhartt built a three-story addition to the Rock Hill Cotton Factory on Chatham Avenue.

He built Mill No. 2 on 100 acres along what was then called Red River Road. Eventually, he increased it to 2,000 acres and used the land for workers' houses. A British architect designed the mill and surrounding area to resemble an English mill

161

village, called Carhartt Station, and later the Town of Red River. Houses were scattered around a pond; about seven still stand on Lynderboro Street.

He also built himself a mansion according to Mary Long's "Yesteryear" a series produced by WNSC ETV. The property had elaborate gardens and a working dairy. Carhartt once offered the house to President Woodrow Wilson as a summer home.

Mill No. 2, which once employed more than 3,000 people, made unfinished denim work overalls. Carhartt designed the bib overall when he worked the railroad and needed pants with lots of pockets. His wife made the first pair.

The company logo was a heart with a car in it. A promotion calendar proclaimed: "The most priceless ingredient of any product is the honesty and integrity of its maker."

By the mid-1920s the textile industry was faltering and Carhartt sold the mill. His last visit to York County was in 1925, according to the ETV series. He and his wife were killed in an automobile accident on the same corner where their daughter was killed.

The mill was sold in 1925 and became idle in the early 1930s. It was just a shell when purchased by Adrienne LaFar's grandfather in the 1940s. The family business owned by David LaFar Jr. and his brother, Dan, not only owned Randolph Yarns, but Bowling Green Spinning and Harden Manufacturing near Dallas, N.C. The brothers also had interests in three North Carolina mills. They made yarn for apparel, home furnishings and industrial products.

In March 2000, the family parted ways. The Dan LaFar branch took Bowling Green; the David LaFar branch took Randolph Yarns. Harden was closed years earlier.

At one time, Randolph Yarns employed 200 people making synthetic yarns and some cotton yarns, said E. D. Maynard, who was plant manager from 1971 until he retired in 1995. He isn't surprised the old mill is being demolished, "The equipment was not updated in the last few years to keep up with the new technical advances that have been made in the textile industry."

LaFar gave the 70 workers two months' pay when she closed the mill in December. "I wanted to support them as long as I could. It was right before Christmas. That was hard, she said. "Some had been there 35 years."

Axel Demolition of Hillsborough, N.C., is tearing the factory down. The work is expected to take another four weeks. Brick is being cleaned and sold along with metal and the wooden beams and flooring. Some textile companies salvaged machines for parts; the rest will be sold for scrap metal.

LaFar hates to have to lose the building, which marks the end of an era for her family. "I cried the last time I was down there," she said. "It's an emotional situation for me. It's been in my family a long time."

York, South Carolina
March 23, 2003

"Enlightened" mill owner employed modern-day perks.
By Louise Pettus

In 1907, Hamilton Carhartt, a Detroit multimillionaire who made his fortune manufacturing work overalls, came South seeking a factory that would serve as an addition to his growing denim empire. Carhartt was the largest manufacturer in the world of work overalls and gloves with a production that exceeded $2 million yearly.

Carhartt found a cotton mill on White Street in Rock Hill that he was able to buy from Sam Friedheim. It was Rock Hill's oldest mill and the first steam-powered cotton mill in South Carolina.

The mill had been incorporated in 1880 under the name Rock Hill Cotton Factory and opened in 1881 with A. E. Hutchison as president. Friedheim had changed the name to Belvedere. Carhartt renamed the plant Hamilton Carhartt Mill. He had other mills in Detroit, Atlanta, Dallas and Liverpool, England.

Carhartt built a winter home on the Catawba River. It was not long before he turned over the day-to-day management of his company to his son, Hamilton Carhartt Jr. and became a resident of York County. In 1912-1913, Carhartt built Hamilton Carhartt Mill No. 2 near the Catawba River on 100 acres of land he purchased from the Childs estate. He added more farmland until he had more than 2,000 acres.

Carhartt's spectacular home on the Catawba River resembled a Swiss chalet done in stucco. Playing the role of gentleman farmer, Carhartt set up Carhartt Farms with extensive dairy operations and a large number of blooded Arabian horses. At Carhartt Station, Hamilton Carhartt Mill No. 2 employed more than 3,000 people. The homes in the mill village were of stucco and resembled scaled down versions of Carhartt's personal residence.

The blue denim manufactured at Mill No. 2 was sent to Detroit where it was cut and finished. On the bib pocket of each pair of overalls there was sewn a small red heart with a representation of a car placed on the heart, thus, "car-heart." According to the stories of the time, Carhartt was originally a railroad worker who was not satisfied with any work clothes then on the market. He told his wife what he wanted and she constructed a pair of overalls with a cut that he liked and with many more pockets than any work clothing then available. Carhartt liked his new overalls so much that he went into business manufacturing exact copies of his wife's work.

By 1920, Carhartt was spending most of his time on his model plantation on the Catawba River. That year, he sent the following telegram to President Woodrow Wilson: "I wish to offer my home on the Catawba River, in the foothills of the Blue Ridge Mountains, with its complete equipment of servants, Arabian saddle horses, automobiles, etc. to Pres. Wilson for his summer White House. It has ample accommodations for everybody." There was no reply.

163

A community house was built at Mill No. 1 in the summer of 1920. The three-story building boasted a reception hall, reading room, assembly hall, a kindergarten, first-aid room, billiard and pool room and a swimming pool that was 40 by 80 feet.

Hamilton Carhartt was considered to be an "enlightened" mill owner. He had cooperated with Mary Frayser and Winthrop College since 1913 by donating mill property for childcare purposes, adult education and recreation programs.

The next year, 1921, was a hard year for cotton textile manufacturers. A post-war depression set in and Carhartt was overextended. He placed his Rock Hill mills in the hands of a creditor's committee. Charles Cobb, a Rock Hill banker, chaired the committee and attempted to sell the properties.

Finally, Cobb sold the Carhartt property to Red River Mills. In 1928, J. H. Cutter of Charlotte took over the Rock Hill mill. A Gastonia mill purchased the mill at the river and Weill Cotton Company took over 1,000 acres of the farm which stretched from the railroad trestle to the bridge (later Celanese Corporation property.)

About this time, Mr. and Mrs. Carhartt were killed in an automobile accident in Detroit. It was at the same street corner that their daughter was killed while taking her children to school. The Carhartts had made their last trip to Rock Hill in 1925.

Rock Hill, The Herald
July 10, 2005
Man tries to save English cottage he once called home
By Sula Pettibon

The four room, European style cottage sits vacant and decaying in a tiny neighborhood off of Celriver Road. Broken glass from the distinctive windows is scattered on the porch floor and paint peels from walls inside. Hedges grow up past the circular roof hiding the house behind a green screen.

The turn of the century house and four others like it on Lynderboro Street sits on land the owners want to sell for industrial development. Don Yarborough of Richburg wants to save just one, the cottage he lived in with his parents, siblings, and grandmother in 1929.

"You don't see a house like this in York County," said Yarborough, 78. "There is not another one like it in Rock Hill."

He and his niece, Roxann James, say they have gotten tentative permission to move the cottage. James has property in Richburg but wants to keep the house near its original location, she said, adding she'd gladly donate it to an agency. They hope to get a grant or donations to help with the $5,500 plus moving costs. We would like the house to stay in this area, said James, 49.

Almost 100 years ago, the house was part of a village built on a 2,000-acre farm owned by Hamilton Carhartt, a Detroit textile millionaire who made overalls, according to Rock Hill historian Louise Pettus. Carhartt owned mills in Detroit, Atlanta, Dallas and Liverpool, England.

He found his way to the area about 1907 and bought the Rock Hill Cotton Factory on Chatham Avenue. Pettus said he renamed it Hamilton Carhartt Mill and built a three-story addition.

Two years later, he built Mill No. 2 on 100 acres along Red River Road. As the property grew, he created a dairy farm and homes for workers.

A British architect designed the mill and surrounding area to resemble an English mill village, historians say. Originally, it was called Carhartt Station and later the Town of Red River.

The houses, some with conical roofs and others with flared gables and stucco, were scattered around a pond. There was a school and perhaps a church and it is believed to be one of the first areas to have running water and sewer.

Carhartt was pretty advanced on that kind of thing, said Pettus. He built himself a mansion on the Catawba River in the style of a huge Swiss chalet with elaborate gardens, she said. The house was offered to President Woodrow Wilson as a summer home. Wilson never responded to the invitation, Pettus said.

Mill No. 2 once employed more than 3,000 people. The company logo was a heart with a car in it.

By the mid-1920s, the textile industry was faltering and Carhartt sold the mill, Pettus said. In 1937, he and his wife were killed in an automobile accident on the same corner in Detroit where their daughter was killed. The mill became idle in the 1930s. Ten years later, it was purchased by David LaFar and renamed Randolph Yarns. It made yarn for apparel, furnishings, and industrial products.

In 2001, the mill was closed and torn down. The mill and the house were included in a 1993 survey of historical properties in York County and the houses could still qualify for nomination to the National Register of Historic Places, said Sam Thomas, director of curatorial services at the York County Culture and Heritage Museums.

The houses have sagging floors and walls, and some are covered with graffiti. One was destroyed by fire.

Yarborough, a retired loom fixer, and his niece decided to save the house early this year. James has sought advice from various historical and preservation societies in York County. She offered the house to the city of Rock Hill for the nearby River Park on Red River Road but hasn't gotten an answer.

They plan to keep knocking on doors while trying not to get discouraged.

"If we can't get people involved, then Rock Hill is going to lose a very unique piece of architecture," James said. "All we'll have is a picture."

ABOUT THE AUTHOR

Pat Grant is a native Rock Hillian. Her love of research and history has resulted in six books on family lines and several local history books. She enjoys teaching history, religion, and ballroom dance classes. Her community involvement has included presidency of the regional Sierra Club, Oakdale PTA, two Charlotte Dance Clubs and founder and president of the area Astronomy Club. She has been active in several genealogical groups, civic and cultural groups in Rock Hill and Charlotte. She has been honored by St. John's Methodist Church, the State Sierra Club, the Astronomy Club, and the New York NAACP for her work efforts.

She retired from Celanese Corporation in Charlotte managing areas in telecommunications, cable management, facilities, and corporate-wide education. She also taught business courses at York TEC for nine years. Her family has blessedly grown to include four great-grandchildren. Family camping with all the family is her pleasure. She is a tent camper, the colder the better.

Made in the USA
Monee, IL
30 August 2023

41863790R00103